John Alexander Joyce

Jewels of Memory

John Alexander Joyce

Jewels of Memory

ISBN/EAN: 9783337092825

Printed in Europe, USA, Canada, Australia, Japan

Cover: Foto ©ninafisch / pixelio.de

More available books at **www.hansebooks.com**

Yours Sincerely
John A. Joyce.

Jewels of Memory.

— BY —

COL. JOHN A. JOYCE,

3150 U Street, Northwest, Washington, D. C.

Author "Checkered Life," "Peculiar Poems," "Zig-Zag," etc.

"Truth is Stranger than Fiction."

WASHINGTON, D. C.:
GIBSON BROTHERS, PUBLISHERS,
1895.

COPYRIGHT,
BY
LIBBIE JOYCE,
May 15, 1895.

Stereotyped by the Maurice Joyce Engraving Company.

DEDICATION.

I dedicate this volume to the American soldier and sailor whose bravery and patriotism on land and sea for more than a century challenges the respect of mankind and will command the admiration of posterity. —*J. A. J.*

PREFACE.

These Jewels from the casket of personal memory I flash over the ocean of literature, trusting that some sparkling rays may attract human hearts when the soul that divined and the hand that fashioned them has vanished like the dews of the morning. —*J. A. J.*

CONTENTS.

CHAPTER I.
Lyon and Jackson... 11

CHAPTER II.
Fletcher and Blair.. 19

CHAPTER III.
Farragut and Porter... 26

CHAPTER IV.
Sheridan.. 31

CHAPTER V.
Sherman... 38

CHAPTER VI.
Grant... 47

CHAPTER VII.
Roscoe Conkling... 51

CHAPTER VIII.
Spinner in bronze... 66

CHAPTER IX.
Samuel Sullivan Cox... 76

CHAPTER X.
George D. Prentice.. 86

CHAPTER XI.
Parson Brownlow... 95

CHAPTER XII.
Father Ryan and Henry Stanton....................................... 104

CHAPTER XIII.
Breckinridge.. 109

INDEX.

CHAPTER XIV.
General Nathaniel Bedford Forrest.................... 118

CHAPTER XV.
"Corporal" Tanner 123

CHAPTER XVI.
The National Capital.................................. 126

CHAPTER XVII.
The Battle of Shiloh—Louisville Experiences.......... 132

CHAPTER XVIII.
Burnside in East Tennessee 143

CHAPTER XIX.
Jim Nelson; A story of Georgia Loyalty............... 149

CHAPTER XX.
Iowa Experience...................................... 157

ORATIONS.
I. Hector. A Newfoundland dog. Kentucky, 1857....... 171
II. Decoration Day 173
III. Emancipation Day................................. 179
IV. A Toast to Woman 184
Poetic Pebbles 187

JEWELS OF MEMORY.

CHAPTER I.

LYON AND JACKSON.

NATHANIEL LYON, of Connecticut, and Thomas J. Jackson, of Clarksburg, Va., were the Puritanical soldiers of the late civil war. A deep religious conviction of patriotism actuated the hearts of these natural leaders, who never faltered in a plan once adopted, but struck the enemy with lightning force and rapidity, accomplishing by audacity what other generals failed in securing by time and numbers.

Lyon was born in the year 1819, graduated in 1841 at West Point, and was killed at the battle of Wilson's Creek, Mo., on the 10th of August, 1861.

"Stonewall" Jackson was born in the year 1824, graduated at West Point in 1846, and received his death wound at the battle of Chancellorville, Va., in May, 1863, dying on Sunday, the 10th of that month.

Both of these military chieftains served as lieutenants in the Mexican war with Scott and Taylor, fought in the same battles for the Stars and Stripes, and were promoted for marked gallantry. After the Mexican war Jackson resigned his commission and took a professorship in the Military Institute of Virginia, at Lexington, where he taught until the shot on Sumter aroused the nation to battle.

At the close of the Mexican war Lyon went to California, served on the Indian frontier with great distinction and afterwards in the Kansas political troubles, commanding at Fort

Riley and taking a leading part in the bloody events that made Kansas a free State.

In May, 1861, Lyon went to St. Louis and took charge of a handful of United States regulars at the arsenal, and, while only a captain, soon rose to the position of brigadier general and took command of the 5,000 or 6,000 volunteers that Blair, Sigel, Fletcher, Cavender, and other patriots had raised to counteract the militia that Governor Claiborne Jackson had assembled in camp at St. Louis with the evident intention of chaining Missouri to the chariot wheels of the Confederacy. Sterling Price and Governor Jackson had a consultation with General Lyon at the Planters' House on the critical situation existing between the State and national authorities. The city officials of St. Louis insisted that Lyon must confine his military movements to the narrow precincts of the arsenal. Lyon replied that the troops of the United States had a right to march anywhere under the flag, and if any man or body of men attempted to interrupt their course destruction and death would be the consequence to the enemy.

On the 14th of May, 1861, while State and national authorities were haggling about policy and precedent, Lyon made a rapid march with his troops to Camp Jackson, located in the western part of the city, surrounded the State militia commanded by General Frost, and demanded an immediate surrender. There was nothing left to Frost but to fight or lay down his arms, and, as the guns of the loyal troops were ready to belch forth a deadly volley, Frost wisely chose the part of discretion and surrendered his 700 men and their munitions of war.

The citizens of St. Louis were terribly excited over the unlooked-for dash of Lyon, and while the prisoners were being marched back to the arsenal some one in the surrounding mob threw stones at a German regiment, which quickly replied with a murderous fire, killing and wounding a number of people.

For forty-eight hours the city was in a wild state of revolution,

"Home Guards" and "Minute Men" watching each other from street corners, dark alleys, basements, cellars, and attic windows. This daring act of Lyon in capturing the State militia saved Missouri to the Union and drew at once the lines between loyal and disloyal citizens. Thus, one brave spirit is the iron hand to splice the timbers of a crumbling State or solidify the breaking arches of a nation.

While Governor Jackson, of Missouri, was doing his best to drag the State into the whirlpool of secession Governor Letcher, of Virginia, was not slow in organizing troops to sustain the Southern Confederacy and enlist the Old Dominion in the war against the Union.

Thomas J. Jackson was the commander of the State militia under Governor Wise when that rugged fanatic of freedom, John Brown, was wounded, captured, and hung at Harper's Ferry, and Robert E. Lee was the commander of the regular troops on that occasion. The firing on the flag at Sumter was but the echo of the scaffold thud at Harper's Ferry and the knell of human slavery in this Republic. Jackson offered his heart and hand to his native State, was commissioned a colonel, and was soon after made a brigadier general of the Confederacy under the command of Beauregard and Johnston. The brigade of Jackson was felt at the first battle of Bull Run, and while McDowell, Sherman, and Burnside attempted to break the gray lines at the celebrated "Stone Bridge" the Confederate troops immediately under Jackson stood like a stone wall.

General Bee, a companion commander of Jackson, in cheering his men into the fight, called their attention to the front and exclaimed, "Look at Jackson and his men, he stands like a stone wall," and from that historic day to the present time the hero of a hundred battles has been known as "Stonewall" Jackson.

During Jackson's life he was the mainstay of General Lee. In 1862 and 1863 he had an independent command and swept up and down the Shenandoah Valley like an eagle, pouncing upon his prey when least expected. At Winchester he dashed against old General James Shields, of Irish and Mexican memory, and for the first time in Jackson's career he was beaten back like an ocean breaker on a rock-bound shore. He, however, foiled and whipped in detail parts of the commands of McClellan, Fremont, Burnside, Banks, and Miles, capturing more than 11,000 men from the latter at Harper's Ferry.

The celerity of Jackson's movements over the passes of the Blue Ridge, through the luxuriant fields of the Shenandoah Valley, over the swollen streams and rolling hills of Maryland bring to mind the active genius of the Great Napoleon, whether leading his soldiers on foot over the bridge of Lodi or hurling his serried battalions against the foe on the plains of Marengo or at the rising sun of Austerlitz.

It was a common belief with the soldiers of "Stonewall" Jackson that his constant prayer and solemn sincerity assured victory on every field, and the Almighty inspired and led their beloved commander. They never doubted a full supply of rations and clothing while any political generals were found in the Valley, and it was a source of amusement that certain Union officers acted as commisariats for the half starved and ragged Confederates. At Malvern Hill, Antietam, Fredericksburg, and down to the fatal night at Chancellorville, in May, 1863, when he received his death wound from an accidental shot, Jackson never faltered in his duty nor doubted the issue while he had a soldier to command. The same inflexible fortitude that signalized his conduct at Cherubusco and Chapultepec in fighting for his country actuated his soul in battling against it. Peter the Hermit and Marshal Ney were never inspired with more lofty courage or religious devotion to duty than Jackson evinced on the blood-stained battlefields of the late war. When dying at Guinea's Station his wife told him the end of life was near. He replied as his last words, "Very good; very good; all right," and thus as a child of destiny he passed into the realms of the vast unknown.

The integrity and valor that characterized the life of Jackson belong to American heroism, and, although he fought for the disruption of the Union, his bravery and genius must be recognized in every land and clime where man battles with man and dies for what each deems the right.

When Jackson's wound was reported, Lee replied, "He is better off than I am. He lost his left arm, but I have lost my right." "Stonewall" Jackson bore the same relation to Lee that Ney held to Napoleon, and, were it not for the accidental stations of the chiefs, I am convinced that the lieutenants would have outshone the luster of their superiors. It is thus unfortunate for a great genius to be born under the shadow of one in a great office, for, while the subordinate exercises wonderful powers, his greatest deeds are obscured by the commanding general, and the glory that should shine out like the mid-day sun beams dimly, like the evening star through the mists the great luminary has diffused!

After the fall of Camp Jackson, in Missouri, General Lyon took immediate command of all the troops in St. Louis, replacing General Harney, whose age and inaction ill suited him for controlling the desperate daily events occurring through the State.

Governor Jackson and General Price had begun hostilities in the center of Missouri, and as no time could be lost Lyon issued his proclamation against the treasonable movements of the Confederates, and marched at once on Jefferson City, the capital of the State. He also sent a force to Southeast Missouri, where a handful of men under Colonel Thomas C. Fletcher turned aside the soldiers of Price at Potosi and prevented the capture of St. Louis.

On the approach of Lyon to Jefferson City the combined Confederates under Sterling Price retreated to Boonville, where a battle was fought on the 17th of June, 1861, resulting in a complete triumph for the Union troops. Lyon followed up his success, pushing the enemy towards Springfield in Southwest Missouri, after defeating them at Dug Springs. The foe finally assembled at Wilson's Creek, about 9 miles from Springfield, where General Ben McCulloch made a junction with Price, massing a force of 24,000 men as against 6,000 under Lyon. The Confederates had a cavalry force alone of 6,000, while Lyon had only 500. Yet, with this great difference in numbers, the worn-out condition of his volunteers, and the heartless and jealous conduct of superiors in failing to reinforce him, General Lyon called a council of war and determined not to retreat and give up all the blood-bought territory that had been recently gained, but to make a night march, attack the enemy at daybreak and risk all that fight and fate might present. The determination of Lyon to attack a force four times his number was worthy the bravery of Alexander or Napoleon, and, were it not for his untimely death in leading the First Iowa to a desperate charge, it is conceded on all sides that the Confederates would have been defeated and driven from the State. The fight continued for nine hours with alternate success. Lyon divided his little army into two divisions, retaining about 4,000 men himself, while Sigel with the remainder and a battery of guns made a detour from the main line of attack in order to strike the enemy on the flank and rear and then rejoin Lyon at a given point, but before Sigel was aware of his location and danger the enemy drew him into ambush, where he lost five of his six guns and a number of his men were taken prisoners, and thus the German general was broken up and crippled during the balance of the battle.

Lyon, however, kept up the fight on the Confederate lines with the most desperate resolve, receiving two wounds, while his horse was killed under him, yet he mounted another and led his last charge, in the midst of which he was pierced through the breast with a rifle ball.

Major Sam Sturgis, of the regulars (late general commanding at the Soldiers' Home in Washington), by common consent took charge of the troops after the death of Lyon and continued the fight into the afternoon, driving the enemy from their camps and off the field. Knowing the superior numbers of the Confederates, Sturgis withdrew to his base of supplies, at Springfield, and turned over his command to General Sigel, who made a masterly retreat to Rolla with all his stores and a quarter of a million of Government money.

The death of Lyon threw a cloud of sorrow over the Union cause, and while his corpse was *en route* to his native Connecticut the people of great cities paid homage to his memory and the Congress of the United States passed resolutions of respect and regret, while eloquent eulogiums were delivered in honor of the fallen hero. When the will of Lyon was opened by his executors it was found that he left his money, more than $30,000, to be devoted to the preservation of the Union; thus giving all, both life and fortune, for the salvation of his flag and country.

Lyon and Jackson were deeply mourned by their friends, and in all human probability had these natural soldiers lived until the last shot at Appomattox they would have been in supreme command of their respective armies. Jackson was mathematical, solemn, and a strict believer in predestination. Lyon might have been the right arm of Oliver Cromwell, and while gifted with the military genius of Jackson he combined statecraft with his war-like talent, and was thoroughly conversant with the political philosophy of the Republic. These warriors had many elements in common. The Puritan of Connecticut had the solemnity of the cavalier from Virginia. Lyon was direct and positive in his work. So was Jackson. The Yankee was spare and angular, with piercing bluish gray eyes. The Southern soldier looked about the same. Lyon was studious. Jackson was contemplative. Lyon never doubted. Jackson was self-reliant. Lyon left West Point as Jackson entered. Each fought for the old flag in Mexico, but when the rebellion began they separated, on the ideal of duty, and fought as earnestly as when bleeding for the same banner. The genius and death of Lyon gave genuine promise of his greatness, while the death of Jackson, nearly two years after, found him the right arm of the Confederacy and in the zenith of his glory. Lyon with a regiment would fight a division. Jackson with a division would fight a corps, and each could command an army.

While Lee and Longstreet, Grant and Sherman, learned wisdom from the rugged road of experience, Lyon and Jackson divined at once the motives of men, planned the attack, struck the blow, and as a natural sequence triumphed where defeat perched on the banners of those who doubt.

The brain of the natural soldier is his map of battlefield. As the pawns, knights, and bishops are moved on a chess board, he organizes brigades, divisions, and armies to checkmate his foe at some central point, and wins the victory while his adversary hesitates on the field of slaughter.

The name and fame of Lyon and Jackson shall emblazon the military pages of this great Republic as long as honesty and valor are respected, and side by side through the coming ages these imperturbable, ideal soldiers shall march in the van of the military heroes who have gone down to universal silence in the crash of battle.

> Peace to Stonewall Jackson,
> God bless brave Lyon, too;
> Sighs and tears we'll mingle
> For the Gray and for the Blue;
> And coming ages yet shall weave
> Fondly, fair and true—
> Garlands bright above the mounds
> Where sleep the Gray and Blue!

CHAPTER II.

FLETCHER AND BLAIR.

GOVERNOR THOMAS C. FLETCHER, of Missouri, was born in Jefferson County of that State on the 22d of January, 1829. His parents were from the Eastern Shore of Maryland and were slaveholders.

A few months' schooling in the fall and winter during boyhood under the ferule of a country pedagogue in an old log school house was the extent of his early education. At the age of twenty-one he was elected clerk of his county and recorder of deeds, and held these positions until 1856, when he was admitted to the bar and resigned the county offices.

Although reared and educated in the atmosphere of slavery he was instinctively opposed to the institution, and when the Republican party was formed in 1856 he was a delegate to the national convention, the first from any slave State. He was a member of the Chicago convention that nominated Mr. Lincoln in 1860, and canvassed his State for the great Liberator.

In personal appearance Fletcher is a fine-looking man. He stands six feet one; stalwart and straight in form. His head is large, round, and high, of Shaksperian proportions. His eyes are dark brown, nose prominent, lips and chin emphatic, yet a contour of countenance expressing benevolence and deep thought.

When he makes up his mind on any private or public subject he stands as firm as the rocks, and no cajolery or threats can intimidate him. He has been a pioneer of thought and leads instead of following, simply because nature built him that way. When others hesitate to go to the front, he is the first to step right up to the danger line and toe the mark, even unto death. He is very politic to a certain point and will do as much for peace, order, and compromise as any man, but when it comes to the word "fire," his pistol goes off first.

I met Governor Fletcher in St. Louis twenty-five years ago, and from that time to this, as a mystic brother, a soldier comrade, a confidential lawyer, and unfaltering friend, we have been on the most intimate terms. Often have I sat in social conclave with himself and friends in St. Louis and Washington and heard his reminiscences of the late war and the great actors in the rebellion.

The winter of sixty and sixty-one, up to the shot on Fort Sumter, was a stirring and fearful period for the loyal men and women of Missouri.

Seated one day, in the fall of 1870, at the Planters' House, in old John King's restaurant, with Fletcher, Francis P. Blair, Gratz Brown, William McKee, Henry T. Blow, and James B. Eads, I heard more early war stories from these noted men than I ever expect to hear again. They have all passed into the vast unknown, save Fletcher, who still lingers as one of the few war governors. On that occasion he was the principal spokesman, although General Frank P. Blair put in his oar every now and then with a deep splash that stirred up the waters of memory.

Fletcher remarked to Blair, "Don't you remember when you took a crowd of us 'roosters' down to the arsenal and introduced us to General Lyon that cold February morning just after his arrival from Fort Riley, in Kansas?"

"Well, I should say so," answered Blair; "when I forget myself I'll forget Nathaniel Lyon, in my opinion the greatest soldier of our war. Yes, boys it will be a cold day when I forget that red-headed Puritan. What a stern, manly-looking officer he was, with his close-fitting captain's uniform, his erect and athletic form, piercing deep blue eyes, Roman nose, thin lips, firm jaw, expressive of indomitable will, and a voice as clear and distinct as the tones of a midnight fire bell."

"Tom," said Blair, "do you know that if it had not been for

that hero, Lyon, Missouri would have been chained to the wheels of the Confederacy, for General Harney was either too partial to the Southern leaders or too inert to know or see what 'Claib.' Jackson and his gang were doing."

"No, Frank, I think if it had not been for your influence with Secretary Cameron and President Lincoln in superseding Harney with Lyon, Missouri might have been for awhile cut away from the moorings of the Union; but, by the Eternal, we'd bring her back or burst the Republic in trying! And, then, you were behind Lyon in urging him on to the capture of Frost and his militia at Camp Jackson!"

"Frank," said Fletcher, "tell us all about that celebrated Planters' House meeting between Lyon and Claib. Jackson."

"Well," said Blair, "there isn't much to tell. It was short, sharp, and decisive. There were only six of us present. 'Claib.' Jackson, the governor; Sterling Price, and Tom Snead represented the Confederate cause, while Lyon, Major Conant, and myself stood out for the Union. Lyon opened the ball by saying that I would do the talking for the Government, as the authorities at Washington had confidence in my loyalty. Governor Jackson first said, 'I do not want the Government to enlist troops in Missouri or march its soldiers across the State.' I could see that the only reason Jackson asked for the conference at all was to gain time and make sure Missouri should enter rebellion. We talked pro and con for about three hours, and the more we talked the further apart we found ourselves.

"I could see by the flash of Lyon's eyes and his compressed lips that he was getting madder and madder as the discussion progressed, and, while he suggested that I should do the talking, he soon took the lead himself and threw out his national ideas like hot shell out of a cannon.

"I saw at once that the fiery captain was about to break up the conference, when, finally, in reply to Governor Jackson, he said: 'Rather than concede to the State of Missouri the right to demand that the National Government shall not enlist troops within her borders or bring soldiers into the State whenever it pleased and move them at its own will into, out of, or through the State; rather than concede to the State of Missouri for one single moment the right to dictate to my Government in any matter, however trivial, I would see (pointing to each of us) you and you, and you and you and you; and every man, woman, and child in the State dead and buried!'

"Then, pointing directly at Governor Jackson, he said: 'This means war! In an hour one of my officers will call and give you safe conduct through my lines.' And then, turning on his heel, without a look or word he rushed out of the room with rattling spurs and clanking saber, the personification of Napoleonic defiance and action.

"We looked at each other in blank amazement for a few moments, made a few personal remarks, when Conant and myself bid good-bye to our Jefferson City friends, and from that moment to the close of the civil war we were open enemies."

The group of men that sat around that festive table I shall never forget. They were leaders, and each in his day played an important part.

William McKee was born in the Empire State and came West when a boy, and soon after engaged in newspaper business. He became proprietor of the old *Union* and was the exponent of Benton, after which he became the proprietor of the *Democrat*, with George Fishback, and afterward the *Globe-Democrat*, with Dan Houser. Under the present editorial management of Joseph B. McCullough ("Little Mack") it has become a power in the land, and its miscellaneous articles and editorials are copied all over the world.

B. Gratz Brown was a brilliant journalist, lawyer, and politician, and in the early contests with slavery he took sides with freedom, and while editing the old *Democrat* he warmly espoused the ambitions of Frank Blair. Brown was a native of Kentucky, became governor of Missouri in the so-called "Liberal" movement that upset the uncharitable and tyrannical "Drake" constitution. He ran as Vice-President on the ticket with Horace Greeley, and both were swamped in a tidal wave of popular indignation, poor Greeley dying soon after as a victim of vaulting ambition.

Henry T. Blow, a wealthy miner and white lead manufacturer, was a citizen of great influence and commanded the respect of personal and political powers. He had been a Congressman, and also represented the United States at the court of Dom Pedro, in Brazil, negotiating commercial treaties with that Empire very advantageous to the country. He was a man of inborn politeness, shrewd, diplomatic, and generous, and was held in the highest esteem by General Grant, who often consulted him about political matters in the West.

Captain James B. Eads was a man of remarkable perseverance and possessed an extraordinary genius as an engineer. His perceptive faculties were largely developed, and his head might serve as a companion-piece to Bismarck or Humboldt.

Sir Christopher Wren and John A. Robling were never inspired by a larger scope of ambition in the profession of engineering and architectural skill than Eads. He was equal to any emergency. When the United States wanted ironclads to ply up and down the waters of the Mississippi during the war, Captain Eads jumped into the arena and filled the bill.

When St. Louis stood halting for many years for bridge connection with the East, with small ferries and a river of ice at its front, it was Eads that came forward and threw across the Mississippi the finest steel bridge in the world, resting on piers and abutments, based on the rock of ages.

When the mouth of the Father of Waters became filled and choked with the sands of centuries, brought down from the golden and silver ribs of the rocky mountains, it was Eads who planned and executed the herculean task of a national dentist, and tore away the snaggled teeth and lumpy roots, giving to the Nation, by his jetties, a free river to the bounding billows of the gulf.

General Francis Preston Blair first saw the light of day at Lexington, Ky., on the 19th day of February, 1821. He sprang from Virginia stock, his grandfather, James Blair, removing to Kentucky in the year 1800, and was afterward attorney general of his adopted State, while his son Francis, the father of our subject, became a noted political character during the life of Henry Clay, Andrew Jackson, and Martin Van Buren, being for many years the editor of the *Congressional Globe*.

The same year that ushered General Blair into the world, Missouri, the theater of his earlier and later triumphs, was admitted into the Union after a hard contest between the Democratic and Free Soil parties, when the celebrated Missouri Compromise forbidding the further extension of slavery was enacted.

Blair graduated at Princeton when only twenty years of age, and settled in St. Louis to practice law. His restless spirit tested the wilds of the Rocky Mountains in 1845 and 1846 until the Mexican war found him with Kearney and Doniphan battling for the old flag.

In 1848 he supported the Free Soil party under the leadership of Van Buren, and in 1854 was elected to the legislature after a very hot canvass on the slavery question. In 1856 he was elected to Congress and made a noted speech favoring the colonization of the black man in Africa, endeavoring to pluck the thorn of slavery from the side of the Republic.

He was a passionate orator and a slashing editorial writer, fearless and manly in all his movements.

When Fort Sumter was fired upon and the flag of the Nation desecrated he was the first man in Missouri to step to the front and offer his services to the Government. For four years he battled on the Mississippi, Cumberland, and Tennessee for the salvation of the Union. He left the Army in September, 1864, after the capture of Atlanta, a major general, who commanded the fighting Seventeenth Corps through all its historic marches and battles.

General Logan and himself took part in the Presidential campaign and rendered invaluable service to Mr. Lincoln and the Republican party.

Logan was a loyal Democrat, and wherever the banner of " Black Jack " moved on the field of slaughter there was found intensity and victory. He inspired his command with the spirit of his own unconquerable soul, and rushing into battle, with long, flowing raven locks, he was the equal of Murat at Marengo, Skobeleff at Plevna, and Sheridan at Winchester. So long as the Grand Army of the Republic, Loyal Legion, and Sons of Veterans exist and Decoration Day, the 30th of May, is celebrated as a national holiday, just so long, in bronze, song, and story, will the memory of our illustrious comrade shine down the crowding ages.

A few years after the war General Blair allied himself with the Liberal-Democratic party, was elected to the United States Senate, and became a candidate for Vice-President on the ticket with Horatio Seymour.

His opposition to the reconstruction laws of Congress was radically pronounced, because of that generous, spontaneous nature that would not hit a man when down.

Blair was six feet tall, high forehead, prominent nose, firm lips, gray eyes, and walked upright through the world as God had made him.

The people of St. Louis have erected a statue to his memory, and, so long as loyalty and Lyon are remembered by the Nation, such patriots as Fletcher Logan, and Blair will find a prominent niche in the temple of the Republic!

CHAPTER III.

FARRAGUT AND PORTER.

For more than a hundred years the American Navy has sustained the honor and life of the Republic, and, although Albion boasts of being mistress of the seas, we have matched her Nelson, Blake, and Cockburn with Paul Jones, Stephen Decatur, and David Farragut.

Wherever the Stars and Stripes met the Union Jack or any other flag, on land or sea, its enemies were finally forced to surrender to the emblem of freedom.

The American soldier at Lexington, Yorktown, New Orleans, and Gettysburg performed heroic deeds of universal renown, yet the American sailors on the Bonhomme Richard, the Chesapeake, the Essex, the Constitution, the Armstrong, the Monitor, the Cumberland, the Kearsarge, and the Hartford has written his name in letters of blood and radiant light on the highest roll of battle glory.

Today, although not first in the list of maritime war vessels, we can, if necessary, with the New York, the Columbia, Terror, and Indiana, commanded by such specimen officers as Admiral Walker, Captain Robley Evans, and Lieutenant Lucian Young, conquer and capture anything that monarchy can send against us. This is not said in any boasting spirit, but with that absolute faith our people have always had in the shrewdness and pluck of the Yankee sailor.

I have participated in war and deeply studied the elements that guarantee victory on land and sea, and I am thoroughly convinced that it is not large forts, big ships, steel plates, or great guns that lead to success in desperate encounter. No; it is the stout heart, the iron nerve, and the unconquerable will beating under the blue jacket, that makes tyranny tremble and waved our glorious flag over the defeat of every foreign and domestic foe.

I was introduced at the White House to Admiral David G. Farragut by General Grant very soon after his first inauguration as President.

The Admiral impressed me as a man of lofty ideals. He spoke in measured tone, looked rugged in form, swarthy, with wrinkles from the sea, and large, dark eyes, inherited, no doubt, from his Spanish ancestors, who were great soldiers and officers in the thirteenth century, and aided their royal master in expelling the Moors from their luxurious abodes on the sunlit slopes of Granada and Andalusia. The father of the Admiral was a soldier in our Revolutionary War, and soon after its close moved over the mountains to the wilds of East Tennessee, where our hero was born at Campbell's Station, near Knoxville, on the 5th of July, 1801.

When only a boy of ten years he was taken aboard of the celebrated Essex by Commodore Porter, where he no doubt, received the first lessons of naval warfare. He rose step by step from the war of 1812 to the rebellion of 1861, when his firm character placed him at the head of the American Navy. He impressed me as a lonely, solemn character who lived in his own world of glory and cared but little for the adulation and flattery of mankind. He seemed wrapped in the solitude of his own originality—a hermit enthroned on the mountain crag of thought.

I have found all great men plain, simple, and unobtrusive, making no pretense whatever, resting their renown and historic greatness upon their blunt deeds. The Admiral was one of this kind, as is well known by his action on the Hartford in passing forts Jackson at New Orleans and Morgan at Mobile.

His fleet advanced on Mobile at 6:47 oclock that August morning, when Captain Alden, the leading officer, suddenly stopped. Farragut, from his high lookout in the rigging of the Hartford, shouted: "What's the trouble?" Alden replied, "Torpedoes!" Farragut exclaimed: "Damn the torpedoes! Four bells, Captain Drayton! Go ahead!"

And, then and there, the Hartford led the line to victory, crowning the old Admiral with a wreath of imperishable glory. His fine statue, made by the artistic Vinnie Ream, now graces the Capitol.

> Glory to great Farragut,
> And to the Hartford true,
> That ploughed through the torpedoes,
> With the red, the white, and the blue!

DAVID D. PORTER.

I met Admiral David D. Porter in the fall of 1874, being introduced by his good wife, who wished to see me relative to a position in the revenue service for her son Essex, at St. Louis. I had never seen the Admiral before and was much interested in such a noted sailor. He seemed to be a man of strong prejudice and indomitable will.

He was born in Chester, Pa., on the 8th of June, 1813, the son of that other David D. Porter that swept the Atlantic and Pacific in the war of 1812, and who made such a wonderful fight in the harbor of Valapairaso against the combined attack of the British war ships Phœbe and Cherub. I could not help while looking on his fine, firm countenance, thinking that "blood will tell," no matter what carping critics may say to the contrary. We conversed for more than an hour upon personal, political, and war memories. I sent an occasional shot to prod and elicit the Admiral's rich and rare reminiscences. I tried for the time to be a good listener, which is a rare faculty. He referred with commendable pride to his naval and army ancestors, who figured prominently in the history of the United States since the Revolutionary war.

By a twist in the talk, I switched him off to a description of the attack on Forts Jackson and St. Philip and the passage of

Farragut's fleet up through the throat of the mammoth Mississippi and on to the final capture of New Orleans in April, 1862. His eyes brightened as I referred to the terrible mortar and gunboat bombardment on the forts and their ready response for six days.

"Yes," he said, "I was placed in charge by the Secretary of the Navy of the mortar and gunboat Flotilla, more than twenty crafts, under the general command of Captain Farragut, to accomplish the destruction of the forts, rebel rams, and gunboats; and the ultimate capture of New Orleans. History will show that such a continuous, red hot, blazing firing, night and day, has seldom if ever been witnessed from frail wooden crafts on a rapid river against seemingly impregnable forts, seige guns, chains, hulks, rams, and fire rafts.

"Yet while the heroic and unconquerable Farragut did not have an ironclad in his whole fleet of forty-six bottoms, he managed to surmount every obstacle and reduced the strongest works of the Confederacy, dealing a blow to the rebel cause that it never survived, and leading the way for General Grant, about a year later, to baffle Pemberton and Johnston and force the surrender of Vicksburg.

"Farragut well knew the boasted strength of New Orleans and its fortified vicinity, but he also knew that with such brave subordinates as Bailey, Bell, Boggs, Morris, Alden, Craven, and Caldwell he could sail or steam through the harbors of hell and make the devil himself surrender!

"About 2 o'clock on the morning of the 25th of April the whole fleet moved up the river to pass the forts, chains, hulks, fire-rafts, and rams that the enemy had prepared for our reception.

"In three hours the grand work was accomplished, after the most desperate conflict I ever witnessed. The morning heavens were lit up, as if volcanic fires and smoke were belching from the bowels of the earth, and the terrible roar of shot, shell, and bombs from forts and river made a perfect pandemonium.

"By 11 o'clock in the morning Farragut flashed the Stars

and Stripes in the very teeth of New Orleans and demanded of Mayor Monroe the surrender of the city and the hoisting of the old flag over the custom-house, mint, and city hall to replace the Pellican flag that still waved after the retreat of General Lovell.

"I was ordered to remain with my mortar and gun boats and force the surrender of Forts St. Philip and Jackson, which I did in forty-eight hours, leaving the latter fort a mass of destruction, in fact a complete wreck, for during the days of the extended bombardment I threw 5,000 bombs and shells into these devoted strongholds of rebellion."

Admiral Porter was at this point interrupted in his extremely interesting story by a message from President Grant, who desired to see him. I reluctantly shook hands and took my departure, but strung another jewel on the sunlit chords of memory!

The old hero now sleeps beside his loyal wife under the shady oaks of Arlington, to the left of General Sheridan and in front of the mansion once inhabited by General Lee. His glorious grave is yet unmonumented, but I trust the Nation will not allow such a gallant warrior to slumber in obscurity, and, ere long, erect over his remains a great granite shaft, firm and conspicuous as the character it will memorize.

Congress should not allow its naval heroes who have passed to the realm of shadows to be forgotten. The corners, angles, squares, and circles of Washington City must be devoted to heroic statues, and, soon as possible, the first to be honored should be John Paul Jones, Stephen Decatur, William Bainbridge, David D. Porter, and William B. Cushing, the desperate young hero that blew up the rebel ram Albemarle, leading thirteen men in the night attack, who were all lost but himself.

A Republic thus honoring the memory of her illustrious sons perpetuates its own life; and, as the Athenians and Romans erected splendid monuments to their heroic dead, so should we rear memorials to the brave men who have fought and fell for the perpetuity of this Republic!

CHAPTER IV.

SHERIDAN.

A FEW days before the battle of Stone River, Tenn., in December, 1862, I first met General Philip H. Sheridan. He commanded an infantry division in the Army of the Cumberland, under the illustrious General Rosecrans. Standing in front of his tent, surrounded by some of his staff, on the edge of a clump of cedars, and looking toward the enemy's camp, Sheridan presented the picture of a typical soldier. He could not have been more than five foot six, and his hair was beginning to show strands of gray, while his grayish blue eyes peered into the distance like a flash from the eye of Destiny. His head was round, forehead high and square, with a punctuation point of a nose surmounting a short mustache, firm lips and emphatic chin that said to all the world, "Clear the track and make room for my command!"

His division did the best fighting at Stone River and saved Rosecrans' right from the repeated onslaught of Hardee and Bragg; and many months afterward, at Missionary Ridge, he led his dashing command over the Confederate breastworks and was the first to plant the Stars and Stripes over the shattered hosts of Bragg and Breckinridge.

When General Grant took charge of the Army of the Potomac, in May, 1864, he cast about for some man of nerve, dash, and judgment to take command of the cavalry and knit together the broken remnants of the various divisions that had become somewhat of a laughing stock with the infantry boys, who repeatedly offered large rewards to any person who would show them a dead cavalryman.

Grant naturally determined to call to his aid Sheridan, who

had been his social comrade in the wilds of Oregon before the war and who had made a mark in the rebellion not inferior to any officer of his rank in the Army. General Mead was in immediate command in the field of the Army of the Potomac, which included the cavalry.

Sheridan soon found that his three divisions were ordered right and left after he crossed the Rapidan, and while virtually in command of all the cavalry would often detach certain divisions and leave Sheridan to do the best he could to foil the movements of Jeb Stuart, the most illustrious cavalry officer of the Confederacy.

Sheridan remonstrated with Mead, and at headquarters on one occasion gave his opinion in no uncertain words and bolted out of the tent with exclamations of insubordination. Mead soon after repeated the incident to General Grant and complained of Sheridan's talk and action. Grant asked him, what did Sheridan say? Mead replied that Sheridan wanted direct and absolute charge of the cavalry, and if he was allowed the privilege he would go right on and whip hell out of Jeb Stuart. "Did Sheridan say that?" "Yes;" replied Mead. "Then," said the General, "I'd let him go out and do it!"

The world has long since known how the hero of Winchester and Appomattox went over the hills and vales of Virginia like the roar of thunder and death-dealing strokes of lightning. He whipped Stuart's cavalry, as he promised, and killed the commander. A Texas blizzard or a West India cyclone were not more deadly in their whirling course than Sheridan when pursuing an enemy, with 10,000 troopers at his back. His eye and mind grasped the situation in all its details and his presence at any one point during a battle was worth 1,000 men.

A few days after the great Chicago fire I visited that city from St. Louis in company with Orville Grant. Sheridan's Sheridan's headquarters were there at the time, and through his active instrumentality thousands of famished citizens received food and shelter. Many bless his memory to this day for the immediate relief furnished by the Government. Half of the city was laid in ashes. While riding about the smouldering ruins with Orville Grant I could see on every hand tents that had been issued by the military arm of the United States to shelter weary and destitute people.

The business house of Grant & McLean, located on Lake street, was destroyed and their stock of leather, harness, and saddles went up in smoke. Orville was $40,000 worse than nothing. He still had his little frame house on Wabash avenue, so far out that the fire failed to reach it. I remained at his house with his wife and four children two days, but before I left assisted him in business.

The evening before I started back to St. Louis, he suggested that we call on General Sheridan, who was privately located in bachelor quarters, on Michigan avenue about four blocks away from the house of Orville. I was glad to accept the invitation, as I had not seen the General since the war and felt that a few hours in his presence could be spent with pleasure and profit. The house was a modern one, plain and well furnished, looking out on the rolling waves of Lake Michigan as they beat in rhythmic tattoo on the sandy beach or dashed over the stony breakwater that stretched away in the glimmering twilight.

Grant and myself were ushered into the parlor, and soon after Sheridan appeared, greeting us with that off hand sincerity that characterized all his movements. We talked for some time about the awful catastrophe that had visted the Garden City, and the General talked and acted as if he had suffered a personal loss in the widespread destruction.

Finally, about 10 o'clock, we made a motion to retire, but he asked us to remain a little longer, while he disappeared for a few moments and then returned. Soon after a servant appeared with a large decanter of brandy and three glasses. He placed the Bacchanalian instruments on a marble center-table and departed. The General asked us to help ourselves, saying: " There is some first-class brandy that a friend sent me. I want you to try it, and if you like it we will have some more." Grant and myself filled our glasses, as did also the General, and we drank his health; and I, to punctuate the toast, included the black horse that he rode at Winchester. Each of us saw the bottom of his glass, and I noticed at the mention of the black horse the General's eyes snapped fire as if he was once again in the saddle, rushing down the pike toward Cedar Creek to turn retreat into victory.

I remarked, General, won't you be kind enough to tell us some of the details of that famous ride of yours that Buchanan Read has immortalized in poetry, and on the spur of the moment I quoted this verse—

> " The first that the General saw were the groups
> Of stragglers, and then the retreating troops.
> What was done, what to do, a glance told him both,
> And striking his spurs with a terrible oath,
> He dashed down the line 'mid a storm of huzzas,
> And the wave of retreat checked its coure there because
> The sight of the master compelled it to pause!"

The General smiled and said: "Joyce, I am afraid the poet did more for Sheridan than he ever did for himself. Read was here some time ago and took dinner with me. That marble bas-relief on the mantel-piece of Rienzi and myself dashing down the Winchester pike was presented by some of his friends. If it had not been for the strength and spirit of that black horse out in the stable, pointing to the rear, I doubt very much whether I'd have got on the field in time to turn the boys back, recover our camps, and thrash Early before dark!

"You may know I had been up to Washington for a day or so to consult with President Lincoln and Secretary Stanton on the situation in the Valley, and left Crook, Wright, Merritt, and Custer to take care of things until I returned, not thinking that Early would take the offensive, remembering the lesson I taught him the month before at **Fisher's Hill.**

"But very early, in fact before daylight, on the 19th of October, an officer came to my temporary headquarters, near Winchester, and reported continuous firing at the front. I had just got back from Washington. I told the officer to find out what he could and report again. I took things leisurely, not thinking but my officers at the front could hold their own with Early in any event.

" Yet, after a hasty breakfast, I became somewhat alarmed at the reports that came in and prepared at once to rush to the front. With Major Forsyth and Captain O'Keefe, of my staff, and about twenty men as an escort, I dashed away from my headquarters through the town of Winchester about 9 o'clock in the morning, leaving Colonel Edwards in command to stop stragglers. I could see from the faces of the citizens, and particularly from the action of the women, that something unusual of good news had reached them by grapevine telegraph.

"After I had crossed over the hill, beyond Mill Creek, I beheld the first view of my panic-stricken army. Hundreds of slightly wounded men, clumps of frightened stragglers, mules, horses, cattle, ambulances, and baggage wagons by the score blocked up the road or dashed about through the fields to find a way to the rear.

"As soon as the boys saw me they threw up their hats, gave some wild cheers, shouldered their guns, and paused in their onward flight. I checked up a moment amid a mob of my broken ranks, took off my hat, gave them a loud cheer and impulsively cried, ' Boys, if I had been with you this morning this thing would not have happened. We must face the other way. We will go back and recover our camps.' They gave prolonged cheers, and I could see that my words of encouragement flushed their eyes and faces with enthusiasm, while the line officers were already endeavoring to bring order out of chaos and reorganize their men for fight.

" I put spurs to Rienzi and once more galloped down the pike through straggling men and broken wagons, through the village of Newton, often leaving the choked-up road for the open fields and cheering the men as I went along, appealing to them to turn back, and I must say they halted to look after me, and their cheers even to this day ring in my ears and thrill my heart.

"Among the first of my generals to meet me was the gallant Torbert, who threw his arms around me and exclaimed, 'My God, I'm glad you've come!' About 10:30 or 11 o'clock I was in the midst of my command, and soon communicated with Crook, Wright, Custer, and Emory, the latter holding the enemy at bay and repulsing many of his frantic dashes. I felt very much humiliated to think that our morning camps on Cedar Creek and my headquarters at Belle Grove House, munitions of war lost; many of my men unburied in front and prisoners in the hands of the enemy.

"Custer and Merritt were forming their cavalry for immediate fight. Wright, Crook, McMillen, and McKenzie, although wounded, were rallying their men. By 1 o'clock in the afternoon I was at the far front, and casting my eyes to the right and left I could see that various regiments and brigades were getting into place and bracing up for defense and a forward movement.

"I intended, in my heart, before night closed down to retake our camps on Cedar Creek and occupy my headquarters at Belle Grove House or boldly sacrifice the balance of my Army. The Nineteenth, Sixth, and Crook's Corps were in good shape at 4 o'clock in the afternoon, and about that time I ordered Custer to lead off in a quick charge to the front and wake up the 'Johnnies,' who seemed to be hesitating as to what they should do with their morning victory.

"My advance was evidently a surprise to Early, and when my infantry got in their murderous work with the crackling roar of musketry I could see that we regained our lost ground rapidly. To make a long story short, by sunset we had the enemy on the dead run across Cedar Creek and far beyond, with thousands of prisoners in our hands, many captured flags, stacks of small arms, transportation material, and more than forty pieces of artillery.

"Well, gentlemen, I must say that I never felt prouder of a day's work in my life than that performed on the 19th of October, 1864. I felt that the power of the rebel army in the Shenandoah Valley was lost forever, and that their supply garden would henceforth furnish food for Union soldiers or be utterly destroyed.

"In winding up my campaign in the Valley I found it a military necessity to destroy some of the mills, grain, and hay that had served the enemy in their rebellion against the Government. For this I have been roundly abused and damned to the echo, but the censure of an enemy I always regarded as praise, and since I satisfied General Grant and President Lincoln, my superior officers, I could well ignore the ravings of the enemies of my country.

"Now, boys, I have told my little story. Let's try a little more brandy, and we'll go out to the stable and pay our respects to Rienzi, the gallant beast that turned defeat into victory at Winchester."

Sheridan stood behind the horse with his hand on his flank, and the noble animal gave a short, low whinny as the General said, "Boys, what do you think of him?" Grant was a fine judge of a horse, and expressed his opinion as an expert. I could see that the horse was jet black, with fine features, clean-cut ears, about sixteen hands high, with strong legs and three white feet, but to my poetic mind I could only see Rienzi as another Bucephalus who would shine down the centuries with his heroic master—

"And when their statues are placed on high,
Under the dome of the Union sky—
The American soldier's Temple of Fame—
There with the glorious General's name,
Be it said in letters both bold and bright:
Here is the steed that saved the day
By carrying Sheridan into the fight,
From Winchester—twenty miles away!"

CHAPTER V.

SHERMAN.

GEN. WILLIAM TECUMSEH SHERMAN was the most brilliant soldier of the late war. He was born in the Buckeye State, where his comrades Grant and Sheridan first saw the light of life ; and, taken altogether, Ohio can count this great triumvirate of illustrious heroes as the best product of her soil.

They were graduates of West Point, and in youth had no wealth or great friends to push them to fortune and fame, but with that pluck and perseverance that characterizes greatness they pushed on to the pinnacle of earthly renown.

Sherman divined the purposes of the Confederate leaders more clearly than any soldier or citizen at the beginning of the war. In January, 1861, before the fire on Sumter, he was president of the Military Academy of Louisiana and had taught the young bloods of the South the science of military movements. Many of his West Point schoolmates circled about his institution, and often at the banquet board he met Bragg, Beauregard, Twigs, Johnston, and the Governor of the State, with his staff, as well as the richest planters and fairest women that the Pelican State could produce. State after State of the South were passing ordinances of secession and wheeling into the vortex of rebellion and raising armies to resist the logic of the election of Mr. Lincoln as President of the United States. Sherman saw and felt the desperate determination of the Southern leaders, and, stating that his fealty and loyalty must forever remain for the Union, he resigned the presidency of the Military Academy and came North to await the overt act of treason. Events were multiplying thick and fast, when, on the 12th of April, 1861, Beauregard shot down the flag floating over Fort Sumter, and on the 14th Major Anderson with his heroic band of loyal soldiers were marched out as prisoners of war, paroled, and sent North. Sherman was in St. Louis at the time and was employed as president of a street railroad company, but was soon after appointed as colonel of the Thirteenth United States Infantry, one of the new regiments called into being by President Lincoln. In June, '61, he was on the staff of General Scott, with headquarters on Seventeenth street, opposite the War Department, but about the middle of July he took command of a brigade located at Fort Corcoran, on the bluffs across the Potomac from Georgetown. He had five regiments and Ayers' battery of artillery. Among the noted regiments of his command were the Seventy-ninth New York, Colonel Cameron's Scotch, and the Sixty-ninth New York, Colonel Corcoran's Irish, who did the best fighting of any of the troops at the first battle of Bull Run, and who formed squares against the "black horse cavalry" and protected the rear on the disorderly retreat of the Union forces to the banks of the Potomac. Colonel Cameron, of the Seventy-ninth, was killed and Colonel Corcoran, of the Sixty-ninth, was wounded and taken prisoner, while his gallant, impulsive Irishmen suffered a greater loss in killed and wounded than any regiment in the division.

Sherman soon after appeared at Louisville, Ky., and relieved General Anderson of the command of the Department of the Cumberland, which he voluntarily relinquished on account of suffocation and nervous prostration that clung to him since the desperate fires of Sumpter. Sherman only stayed in command about two months and was relieved by General Buell. The story was sent afloat through the New York *Tribune* and Cincinnati *Commercial* that he was insane, crazy, etc. This fool roorback arose out of a council of war held at the Galt House for the purpose of talking over the situation in Kentucky and the absolute and immediate need of more troops against the advancing forces of General Buckner and Gen. Albert Sidney Johnston, who were within a day's march of the Ohio River.

Simon Cameron, the Secretary of War, his Adjutant General Lorenzo Thomas and official party were present at the conference. Sherman had then only about 18,000 men, while the enemy had at least 50,000, and he, in that square, blunt manner, informed the Secretary of War that 60,000 men were needed immediately to protect the center of the grand Union line from East to West, and that before Kentucky, Tennessee, and Georgia could be redeemed from rebel sway it would take more than 200,000 men! Cameron jumped from the bed where he he was reclining and exclaimed, "My God! where are you to get the men?" Sherman replied that there were thousands in the North ready to enlist and fight, and it was the business of the War Department to equip them and send them to the front. This shot staggered "Simple Simon" and his adjutant general, who left that afternoon for Washington, and in a few days we only heard of "Crazy Sherman" on the outskirts of Halleck's staff in Missouri, and then on leave of absence with his family at Lancaster, Ohio. But the restless spirit of this loyal, prophetic, heroic warrior could not be cribbed, coffined, or confined by the jealous midgets of mediocrity or the barbed arrows of journalistic gerrymanders. We soon find him in command of Benton Barracks, at St. Louis; then at Paducah, and after the capture of Fort Donelson moving up the Tennessee on transports with a newly-formed division, composed of four brigades, mostly raw troops from the rural districts of Ohio, Illinois, and Indiana. He picked out his camping ground near Pittsburg Landing, three miles out on the Corinth road, where Albert Sidney Johnston was collecting an army to crush the Union forces; and around the gray eagle Sherman more than 40,000 Union soldiers collected under the command of General Grant, and finally won one of the most decisive battles of the war.

I shall never forget the Tuesday morning after the fight as I strolled over to Sherman's division and beheld the hero perched on a stump making one of the most scorching speeches I ever heard. It seemed that in the Sunday fight Hildebrand's and

Buckland's Ohio brigades gave way at the first onslaught of the dashing enemy, and many of the regiments were literally torn to pieces and scattered during the balance of the conflict. Sherman was trying to collect the remnant of the officers and men of these brigades, and this is about the way he addressed the soldier mob that listened to him with the deepest humiliation : " You are a nice set of soldiers. Many of your officers acted like dastard cowards, and I have no doubt that some of them are now feeding fish in the Tennessee River or making tracks for their homes in the North. I'm ashamed of you, and instead of running away from these infernal rebels and dragging your general after you, you should have stood like men and died for that splendid flag that waves over that tattered tent. What in the devil did you enlist for if it was not to fight and die for the Union. Far better had you remained in your father's field hoeing potatoes, pulling pumpkins or at the counter measuring tape or sanding sugar than act in such disgraceful manner before the enemy. Had all the boys done as you did we'd be already *en route* for Libby prison or Andersonville. You must always remember that we hail from the grand old pioneer State of the Northwest, the land of Mad Anthony Wayne, Joshua Giddings, Tom Corwin, Ben Wade, and Gen. William Henry Harrison, and hereafter in battle I want you to die first and run afterward! I intend to have some of your officers dismissed from the Army, and had I my own way I would order now a drum-head court-martial and have at least a half dozen of them shot! Look around you this morning, after the battle, and see your comrades in clumps under the branches of these torn oaks sleeping, in death, the long sweet sleep of heroic warriors. Hereafter imitate their glorious example and in future fights stand like a rock against the enemy, striking to the death for God and your native land!"

This was the most remarkable speech I ever heard, and I inwardly congratulated myself that I belonged to the Twenty-fourth Kentucky and not to any of the regiments that ran away.

His speech was received in somber silence, and the rain from the dripping branches, mingling with the moan of the April winds, were the only sounds that disturbed this military philippic.

We, of course, know that General Sherman rose step by step by the greatness of his own genius. Along the Mississippi, on to Vicksburg, Missionary Ridge, Knoxville, and his great march from Chattanooga to Atlanta and the sea, reminds the historic and intelligent reader of the career of Alexander the Great, who ascended the throne of Macedon and Greece when only twenty, and conquered the eastern world at the age of thirty-two. With 40,000 Greeks he invaded Asia and Persia, and, after a series of desperate battles, on to Arbela, Granicus, and the Indus. He routed and conquered more than 1,000,000 men led by the voluptuous and illustrious Darius and placed the petty potentates of the Oriental world under his feet. The march of Sherman from Chattanooga to the sea, and the rapid, continuous skirmishes and battles through Georgia from the 5th of May, 1864, to the 22d of December, when he rode triumphantly into the city of Savannah, equal in rapidity and importance the movements of the illustrious Macedonian.

I'll never forget a midnight, morning, personal experience I had with the General and Colonel Dayton, of his staff. It was two days before the assault on Kenesaw Mountain, where Joe Johnson had strongly intrenched himself and awaited the attack of his antagonist, the great flanker. My regiment, the Twenty-fourth Kentucky, had been skirmishing through the afternoon and even after sunset on the extreme right of our line, only Stoneman's cavalry hanging around our flanks. When night closed with desultory musketry firing, my regiment, which occupied the right of Cox's division and Cameron's brigade, threw out a strong line of skirmishes along the Sandtown road and near Olley's Creek, where General Schofield, the commander of the Twenty-third Army Corps, had established his headquarters.

I was adjutant of the Twenty-fourth Kentucky at the time, young and enthusiastic, caring little for consequence and less for sleep. About two o'clock on the morning of the 25th of June, while a drizzling rain pattered through the trees on the slumbering soldiers, wrapped in their gum blankets, I rose from a fitful slumber and concluded to go to the front and see how the officer of the day and the pickets were doing their duty. I was tired and hungry, but as we were on the eve of battle I wanted to be on the alert for the benefit of the regiment and not let the "boys in gray" get the bulge on us. With haversack, canteen, coffee can, and gum poncho I quietly made my way through the sleeping regiment, passed the guards, and in a short time reached the picket line, where I found Captain Barber, the officer of the day, making his rounds of a half mile in conjunction with his brother officers of the brigade. In passing back to the regiment near a brook with abrupt banks I met John Caldwell, Jim Jackson, and Reube Warner, of my regiment, standing picket, the extreme infantry outpost of Sherman's army. I saw that under a jutting rock the boys had made a smudge fire to heat up some coffee. I remonstrated with them for the recklessness of the thing, knowing that the enemy were just across the creek, not 500 yards away. However, I told Coldwell to move out some fifty yards farther and I would tend to the cooking of the coffee, for I was nearly famished myself. I dodged behind the rock, took off my own coffee can, filled it with water and coffee, set it on the fire with the other two cans, and began to pile on some dry pine twigs that I found at the root of a tree. It was not long until the coffee began to boil, and my heart went out to the aroma it exhaled. At this moment I heard Warner exclaim, "Halt! who comes there?" The response came, "A friend with the countersign." "Dismount, advance, and give the countersign." A tall form with slouch hat and poncho cape advanced, gave the countersign, as did also his companion. I stepped up immediately and saluted the General and his aid, who knew me personally. Sherman asked me if all was well. I told him that every man was at his post and ready for a fight. I stood between the smouldering fire and the General, to prevent him from seeing the situation, but his lynx eyes and distended nostrils could not be deceived. He said, "Adjutant, how is this? Have you not strict orders that no fires shall be made in front of the enemy?" I replied that what he saw was only a semblance of a fire, and not a fire, and what he smelt was only a couple of cans of coffee that the boys had put on to warm. "Let me see how warm that coffee is." I stepped to the smouldering fire and brought him my can of coffee, which was red hot, and as black as your hat. He took hold of the wire bail, lifted it to his lips very carefully, took a mouthful, and said, "Here, Dayton, take a dose of that." The aid complied to his sorrow, and with a grimace that said, "Oh! hell," passed the can back to the General, who poured out a small part of the coffee and asked me to fill it up with water from my canteen. I did so, and then the General drank two-thirds of the contents, passed the balance to Dayton, who finished it. They mounted their horses, and as the General turned to the rear, said in a half quizzical tone: "Remember, 'boys,' no fire in camp, but at the enemy!"

Inside of forty-eight hours after this interview the corps of Thomas, McPherson, and Schofield were moving to the front and tightening their lines of steel around the rocky ribs of Kennesaw Mountain. Wave after wave of bluecoats dashed against the fortified stronghold of Gen. Joe Johnston, and for nearly three hours Sherman tried in vain to dislodge the foe, and finally drew away to the right flank, which caused the retreat of the enemy to the Chattahoochee River and the fortified surroundings of Atlanta. The battle of Kennesaw Mountain was the first repulse that Sherman received in his grand march to the sea and taught him the lesson not to attack insurmountable heights when he could flank to right or left and accomplish the same result with less loss of limb and life.

I was shot through the upper right thigh in this engagement while leading my regiment against rifle pits at the base of this mountain, and thus received a leave of absence from the Army from that 27th of June, 1864.

I met General Sherman several times after the war in Washington, St. Louis, and New York in social and Grand Army banquet boards. In June, 1875, the General had his headquarters on Olive street, St. Louis, having removed from Washington on account of some disagreement with General Belknap, then Secretary of War.

I called at the General's office one morning to buy a copy of his "Memoirs," that had just been issued from the press of Appleton & Co., of New York. A pile of the books lay on his desk. I expressed my desire to purchase the two volumes, and asked him to put his name on the fly leaf. He immediately picked up his pen and wrote the following phrases:

Inscribed to my friend and fellow soldier, Lieut. Col. John A. Joyce, who bears an honorable wound received at Kennesaw.

With the compliments and best wishes of—

W. T. SHERMAN, *General.*

ST. LOUIS, MO., *June* 24, 1875.

I shook hands with the General, passed through the office, lingered a few moments to chat with his staff—the genial and handsome Audenried, the brave and heroic Tourtelott, and the gallant Whipple.

More than eight years afterward, when the General had retired from the Army, I sent him a copy of my book, "A Checkered Life," and received from him the following letter:

912 GARRISON AVENUE, ST. LOUIS, MO.

Col. JOHN A. JOYCE, *Georgetown, D. C.:*

I thank you for remembering us in the distribution of your most interesting volume, entitled "A Checkered Life." So far as the military events therein described, which have fallen within the span of my personal observation, they are wonderfully accurate. Your poetic flights and fancies are not in my line, but they surely give great interest to your book.

As you know, I have always wished you well and all the happiness possible in life, to which end the respect of your neighbors and acquaintances is a large factor.

I am now out of public office and can look with philosophic composure on the great amphitheater of life, ready to laugh with the audience or to cry in sympathy with the wronged and afflicted.

Yours, sincerely, W. T. SHERMAN.

GEN. JOHN M. SCHOFIELD.

Gen. John M. Schofield was born in Chautauqua County, N. Y., September 29, 1831, and graduated from West Point in the class of 1853, being assigned to the artillery.

In May, 1861, just after the fire on Fort Sumter, he became chief of General Lyon's staff and operated through the early fights for freedom in Missouri and distinguished himself at the battle of Wilson's Creek, wearing a medal of honor for special gallantry.

General Schofield commanded the Department of the Ohio throughout the year 1864 and rendered valuable service to General Sherman in his campaign against Gen. Joseph E. Johnston through the swollen waters and rugged mountain passes of Tennessee and Georgia.

I was introduced to him personally by Gen. J. D. Cox, my division commander, at the battle of Resaca and noticed his coolness and persistency down to the 27th of June at Kennesaw Mountain, where I received my discharge from the United States service. The Confederates, no doubt, fully intended to make me an angel, but through some inscrutable Providence I have been left over to write poetry for the edification of a suffering nation!

General Schofield fought the battle of Franklin, Tenn., on November 30, 1864, one of the bloodiest fights of the war for the number engaged in action. The Confederate general, John B. Hood, whom I knew in boyhood at Mount Sterling, Ky., opposed Schofield, and, while he fought desperately for his cause, suffered a terrible defeat, losing 1,750 killed, 3,800 wounded, and 700 prisoners, while the entire loss of the Union Army in killed, wounded, and missing was only 2,300! Soldiers alone can understand this great defeat and victory.

General Schofield is a well-rounded man, very firm, but kind to those who do their duty, and while he may not rank with Grant, Sherman, and Sheridan, he has convinced his grateful country that he is large enough to wear the shoulder-straps of a Lieutenant General and will wear them with dignity and unsullied honor.

CHAPTER VI.

GRANT.

ON THE corner of Thirty-second and U streets, West Washington, D. C., four blocks west of Oak Hill Cemetery, stands a large double brick mansion on the top of a hill 250 feet above the level of the Potomac. Two acres and a quarter of land belong to the place, and the house sits amid cedars, pines, maples, oaks, vines, flowers, and shrubbery, where the breeze of summer and keen blasts of winter play hide and seek and birds of rare plumage sail and sing. Here I have lived for twenty years.

Colonel Scott, of South Carolina, built the house, but when the late war began he and his family went South and left the property in the hands of Josiah Dent, late Commissioner of the District of Columbia. In 1863 and 1864 the house became the headquarters of General Halleck. When he retired from the command of the Army General Grant came East, with his family and staff took possession of the mansion, while the General was winding up the rebellion.

Looking south through the sunlit atmosphere twenty miles away, you behold one of the most beautiful scenes around Washington. Far to the right can be seen the rolling hills of the Old Dominion and the Chain Bridge, capped with the variegated colors of spring or autumnal hue, stretching away toward Leesburg and the sparkling waters of the Shenandoah. To the front you behold Fort Meyer, Arlington, Fort Runyon, and the famous Long Bridge spanning the Potomac, then on to Alexandria, Fort Foote, Fort Washington, to the tall hilltops of Mount Vernon To the left is Washington, stretching away in artificial and natural beauty, with the great white Monument and the Capitol shining in the golden sunlight of departing day.

I first met General Grant at the battle of Shiloh in the presence of Generals Buell, Sherman, and Rawlings. I was at the time a lieutenant, and was introduced by my colonel, L. B. Grigsby. Grant was then in the flush of manhood, and as the sun struggled through the towering tree tops of that battlefield, Monday morning, the General ordered an advance to regain the ground and victory lost the previous day.

As Grant sat on his horse with hopeful, compressed lips, and sphynx-like countenance, he brought to my historic mind Alexander at the Indus, Cæsar at the Rubicon, or Napoleon at Waterloo. The world since then has been filled with his fame. In after years I knew him well during his political career.

One of the most interesting social scenes I ever participated in was at the home of General Harney, in St. Louis, during the Presidential campaign of 1872. President Grant and family, with General O. E. Babcock, his intelligent private secretary, and his valet Jerry visited St. Louis during the campaign and were entertained by William H. Benton, John F. Long, General Harney, and others.

One evening a fifty-plate feast was given by General Harney in honor of the President. I was present on the occasion, and at the conclusion of the banquet, about 11 o'clock, when the guests had retired to their homes, I was asked by Babcock to walk in the smoking room and wait awhile.

Soon after, General Grant, with General Harney, Judge Treat, Governor Reynolds, George Fishback, Fred Grant, and Babcock put in an appearance and took seats. The cigars were passed around, most of the guests partaking of the fragrant Havanas. The dinner had been greatly enjoyed and satisfaction seemed to sit on each countenance. A flood of old war memories began to run from "Long Knife," as Harney was called by the Indians. He was the hero of five wars—Florida, Creek, Black Hawk, Mexican, and Civil. He described many of the desperate scenes encountered, and thrilled us with patriotism and admiration, and wound up with the request that

General Grant would tell us something about himself at Vicksburg, Donelson, Shiloh, the Wilderness, and Appomattox.

It was then nearly 12 o'clock. Grant swung back in his easy chair, crossed his legs, puffed his cigar and, through circles of smoke that hung about his brow, discoursed about his military career for nearly two hours. He spoke of the trials and scenes of early life, his resignation from the Army, the personal hardships he encountered after marriage, his search about St. Louis for employment, his daily disappointments, clerking in the leather store at Galena with his brother Orville, and, taking the talk all in all, I never heard a more fluent or interesting reminiscence. He spoke of his capture of Fort Donelson and the surrender of Buckner, stating that one of the impelling motives for demanding an immediate and unconditional surrender was the fear that General Halleck might do something to change his plans before the victory in sight could be scored. I could see that his love for Halleck was not as close knit as that between Damon and Pythias.

Speaking of Sherman's protest against his plans for the assault on Vicksburg, he laughingly remarked that "Tecump" did not know all the details; and after the place was captured, he called Sherman to his tent, handed him the written protest that he forgot (?) to forward to the War Department. The two friends had a good laugh over the incident and closed their social chat with a bumper from an old canteen to the surrender of proud Pemberton.

I never met a man with a higher sense of duty than General Grant. His mind acted on direct lines and no amount of verbal sophistry could twist him from a purpose once formed. He was eminently self-reliant, and no storm clouds of misfortune could shadow his mind or chill the intensity of his determination.

When others hesitated, he acted. When trembling mortals fled, he stood like a rock, and when his bravest generals gave up the fight he moved forward to victory.

Before engaging in battle or campaign he calculated all the strength of the enemy and studied the details of the movements he proposed on the chess board of war, acquainting himself particularly with the topography of the contemplated battlefield, and parceling out to each of his generals the work they must do. When he moved against General Lee across the Rapidan and on through the dark entanglements of the Wilderness he made no calculation for retreat, but knew and believed in his own mind that victory would perch on his banner as sure as the sun and stars shone in the heavens. He had the living tools to batter down the walls of the Confederacy, and he used them with a direct and desperate persistency until the fabric of the rebellion fell forever into the bloody waters of the Appomattox.

> A thousand years of glory
> Shall immortalize his fame
> With a tale in song and story
> To keep green his hallowed name:
> How he saved a lasting Temple,
> So complete in every plan,
> For justice, truth, and mercy
> And the liberty of man!

CHAPTER VII.

ROSCOE CONKLING.

ROSCOE CONKLING was an imperious character. His nature was commanding and the midgets of mankind that he managed for so many years were only rounds in the ladder of his lordly ambition. Policy and pelf found no place in the calendar of his philosophy, while principle was the guiding star of his life and truth the touchstone of his soul.

His manly mien, sonorous voice, flashing eye, graceful gesticulation, and satirical tongue cut like a scalping knife, beat back his enemy in forensic debate like the vipers of the Furies, hissing defiance and challenge to combat.

Cowards might compromise for cash and power, but he held in supreme contempt and scorn the man who would not fulfil his pledge and stand out in the broad sunlight of public opinion. Vacillation and subterfuge found no anchorage in the harbor of his heart. Like Napoleon at the bridge of Lodi he dismounted in desperate action, grasped the flag of his party, and dashed to the front through the bullets of the foe, securing victory from the jaws of defeat.

Senator William B. Allison, of Iowa, in whose office I studied law, introduced me to Mr. Conkling in the winter of 1866, when each occupied seats in the House of Representatives. From that time until death closed his illustrious career I knew the great leader of the Empire State.

Politicians follow the trend of public opinion and mould it for their own use. Conkling led it for the glory of a Nation, swaying the multitude by his matchless eloquence. They were politic and diplomatic. He was sincere, sarcastic, and lofty. They gave their word and smile to the many; he gave his heart to the few. While the former had cheering, impulsive followers, he had admiring worshipers. Others came down from their place of power to mingle with the rushing crowd, laughing with and throwing arms around controlling constituents. Conkling stood upon an exalted pedestal like the oracle at Memnon, gazing proudly at the passing throng, expecting genuflections and worship, at long range, from the multitude of mediocrity that listened to and absorbed the decrees that fell from his trenchant tongue. He possessed the bravery of Coriolanus, the beauty of Alcibiades, and the wisdom of Pericles. He had the lashing sarcasm of Danton, the sardonic sneer of Swift, and the sententious sentences of Mirabeau, rising above the petty politicians of the hour and soaring into the realm of statesmanship like an Alpine eagle above the vulture of the valley!

Roscoe Conkling was born at Albany, N. Y., on the 29th of October, 1829. His progrenitors were from Nottinghamshire, England. The father of Roscoe was born at Amaganset, N. Y., graduated at Union College, became district attorney, member of Congress and for twenty-seven years sat on the United States district bench for New York.

The mother of Roscoe was related to the late Chief Justice Cockburn, of Great Britain; was a noted heiress, beauty, and in youth was called "the belle of the Mohawk vale," the original of the celebrated sentimental song. Thus may be seen that Roscoe Conkling inherited wisdom and beauty.

When Conkling was nine years of age his parents removed to Auburn, the home of the celebrated statesman, William H. Seward, who was an intimate friend of Judge Conkling. For three years Roscoe went to the town school and was noted for his stalwart body and mind, a lusty, rollicking, proud boy, who kicked over many senile rules, yet invariably knew his lessons, being endowed with a marvelous memory.

In 1842 he was placed in the classic academy of Prof. Clarke, of New York City, and for nearly four years pursued his varied studies, paying particular attention to history, poetry, and oratory. In 1846, when only seventeen years of age, the family removed to Utica, where Roscoe was entered as a student in the office of Spencer and Kernan, one of the most prominent law firms in the Empire State. He received his license to practice before he was of age, and was appointed district attorney of Oneida County by Governor Hamilton Fish. A few years later he was elected mayor of Utica over a noted Democrat, making a brilliant canvass. He was employed in prominent criminal and civil cases, and often triumphed over his legal tutors. In November, 1859, he was nominated and elected to Congress as a Republican, and took his seat on the 5th of December.

Thad. Stevens, Morrill, Burlingame, Grow, Winter Davis, Sherman, and Corwin were his legislative partisans, while Pendleton, Vallandingham, Cox, Holman, Barksdale, of Mississippi; Pugh, of Alabama, and Reagan, of Texas, were his opponents; yet not one of this list, considering his years of twenty-nine, could lay claim to being his superior in courage or magnetic eloquence. Conkling was re-elected to Congress by a majority of 3,563.

On the last day of February, 1861, the House of Representatives passed an amendment to the Constitution guaranteeing perpetuity to slavery, and many Republicans through fear or to placate the slave oligarchy voted to chain freedom to the chariot wheels of slavery. A Spartan band, however, voted an emphatic "No!" and among them we find Thaddeus Stevens, Tom Corwin, Owen Lovejoy, and Roscoe Conkling.

The Morrill tariff act was passed two days afterward, providing for war taxes and loans and particularly declaring that the Republic is a Nation, not a league, and that it is supreme within its own constitutional sphere.

On the 12th of April Fort Sumter was fired upon, and the echo of the shot was heard around the world, sounding the death knell of slavery and State rights, although at the expense of two millions of men.

In one of Conkling's early war speeches he uttered the following patriotic sentiment: " For one I am for the Union and the Government unconditionally. Come what may I would rather see the rebel cities smoke; I would rather see New Orleans the bed of a lake where fishes would swim; I would rather see the seats of treason unpeopled from the Potomac to the Gulf than that one star should be blotted from the flag of our fathers or one stripe torn from its azure folds ! "

The Ninety-seventh Regiment, New York Infantry Volunteers, or the " Conkling Rifles," commanded by Col. Charles Wheelock, was among the first to respond to the call of the Government for troops to put down the rebellion. Mr. Conkling took a great interest in this regiment, as it was raised from the stout yeomanry of Oneida county. On its departure for the front he presented the regiment with a stand of colors that had been embroidered and fashioned by his patriotic wife, who was the intellectual sister of Horatio Seymour, the standard bearer of Northern Democracy.

The fall and winter of 1862 was a terrible time for the administration of President Lincoln, the Congressional elections in many districts going Democratic, through the persistent howl of " Copperheads," " Doughfaces," and " Knights of the Golden Circle," people who declared that the war was a failure and demanded peace at any price. But Lincoln met the emergency, and in the face of political defeat issued his immortal proclamation, the keystone to the arch of liberty, calling for millions of bondsmen from the gloom of slavery to the God given sunlight of freedom.

In this election Conkling was defeated by 98 votes in a total of 19,788 by his old law preceptor, Francis Kernan; and Horatio Seymour, his brother-in-law, was elected Governor of New York.

For the ensuing two years Conkling practiced law with eminent success, defeating his most prominent opponents in the criminal and civil courts. In the November election of 1864 he was sent back to Congress with a majority of 1,150 votes.

Lincoln, too, was triumphantly elected over McClellan and his mongrel supporters.

In May, 1865, Mr. Conkling was employed by Secretary Stanton to assist the Judge Advocate General of the Army in prosecuting Assistant Provost Marshal General Haddock of the western district of New York, at Elmira, charged with a gigantic conspiracy to defraud the Government out of bounties given to substitutes in the Army. More than a half million of dollars was divided by corrupt lawyers, township agents, county judges, and bounty jumpers.

Mr. Conkling entered the trial as special counsel, and convinced many people that officers high in authority in the provost marshal's office at Washington, as well as prominent politicians, were linked with Haddock and his conspirators. Judge Smith, of Oneida County, became counsel for his friend Haddock, but when he volunteered to take the stand as a witness in behalf of his client the judge literally and abjectly broke down. Conkling proved from Smith's receipts and orders that he accepted bribes while holding the office of county judge. The closing speech of Conkling cut to the bone and drew blood with every sentence.

The court marshal rendered a verdict that Major Haddock be cashiered, pay a fine of $10,000, and be imprisoned for five years. This sentence was carried out by order of Secretary Edwin M. Stanton, the unrelenting Carnot of the late war, whom praise could not inflate or censure depress, a man who soared over difficulties like an eagle swooping over mountain crags.

In November, 1866, Conkling was re-elected to Congress by an increased majority, and for the succeeding two years took active part in the enactment of reconstruction laws, made necessary by the status of the Southern States at the close of the rebellion. He took a very active part in the proceedings for the impeachment of Andrew Johnson, and was a staunch lieutenant to Mr. Thaddeus Stevens, the great radical leader from Pennsylvania.

At the beginning of the war Johnson, like Parson Brownlow, was compelled to leave Tennessee and become fugitives, because of their loyalty to the Union. Johnson then said, and I heard his speech in Kentucky, that "treason must be made odious and traitors punished," but in the whirligig of time he consorted with those he reviled and rebuked the Union people who made it possible for him to become President by the unfortunate assassination of the immortal Lincoln. Parson Brownlow kept his faith to the last, defying the censure of neighbors, the isolation of exile and the torture of imprisonment; a man of heroic and indomitable principle, that no earthly influence could subdue or twist from the moorings of his God given faith!

The impress of Conkling's radical mind can be found in the thirteenth, fourteenth, and fifteenth amendments to the Constitution and the laws enacted for their supremacy. He served on the most important committees of the House and Senate. The slave and freedman found in him an uncompromising champion, and his hand was always extended to prostrate humanity.

Ingersoll in his Albany eulogy of Conkling expresses the ideal of the statesman. "We rise by raising others and he who stoops above the fallen stands erect!"

Lincoln, Grant, Chase, Stevens, Corwin, and Stanton had the highest respect for the New York statesman, and put him forward in the most desperate emergencies, knowing that he was equal to any ordeal of brain or body. Like a gladiator in the Roman arena he stood erect, bared his arm and breast to man or beast, and with javelin or battle axe conquored his foe and commanded the shouts of the multitude.

Conkling took his seat in the Senate March 4, 1867, and resigned the same on the 14th of May, 1881, after fourteen years of illustrious service. His speeches on the hustings, in the Senate, and at conventions of his party, are masterpieces of convincing logic. When Conkling was announced for a set speech in the Senate every seat was filled and the steps in the aisles were crowded. He dressed in clean cut style, and his commanding presence, with Hyperion locks, bore the stamp of an Apollo, and hurled at his opponent the lofty and sarcastic logic of Cicero or Grattan. He was the peer of Thurman, Sumner, Lamar, Morton, Gordon and Hill, and often crossed intellectual swords to the utter discomfiture of these noted men. I heard him in the "French Arms" debate and "San Domingo" question, and such a lashing inflicted on the tender backs of Sumner and Schurz I never witnessed before. Although these Senators were famous masters of language and logic, they utterly wilted and shivered under the political castigation inflicted by the administration Senator from New York. General Grant had in Conkling a lofty and dignified champion worthy the hero of Appomattox, and his speech in nominating Grant for a third term at Chicago will long be remembered by the 306 that followed in his lead as well as those who were fortunate enough to hear the great orator from the Empire State.

The Electoral Commission was evolved and consummated by the brain and energy of Roscoe Conkling, and I doubt very much if Rutherford B. Hayes would ever have been President had not the fine "Italian" hand of the New York statesman taken part in the compromise that continued Mr. Tilden in the shades of private life. It was the first time in our Republic that the constitutional machinery for the inauguration of a President was suspended by a political enactment. Let us hope it may be the last.

Roscoe Conkling refused the position of Chief Justice of the United States, tendered by his faithful and enduring friend President Grant, preferring to legislate for a Nation rather than sit for life on velvet cushions, the *ninth* part of a judicial conclave. Patrick Henry, of Virginia, refused the same office from the hands of President Washington; and these two illustrious orators were the only Americans that cast aside one of the highest offices on earth. However, they were greater than the office, and showed it by their declination!

President Garfield would not have carried the State of New York in 1880 had not General Grant and Roscoe Conkling taken the political field in his behalf, and the loss of New York would have been the loss of the Nation. Conkling, at the written invitation of Garfield, visited him at Mentor during the Presidential campaign and received the most exact and seemingly sincere thanks for his support. In meeting the New York Senator, in the presence of General Grant, Garfield rushed out bareheaded from his home and exclaimed:

"Conkling, you have saved me! Whatever man can do, that will I do for you!" And he did it, by turning General Merritt out of the New York custom-house and putting in General Robertson, the enemy of Mr. Conkling. *Punica fides!*

It matters little now as to who was right or who was wrong in the internal war between contending Republican factions. The "Stalwart" and the "Half-breed" have long since slept beneath the sod, and over their illustrious ashes let us exclaim with the ancients, *nil de mortius nisi bonum.*

The following personal reminiscences clustering around Mr. Conkling may not be uninteresting to the reader, being related for the first time:

The Presidential campaign of Grant in 1872 was a memorable one. Greeley had been nominated by the Democratic party and a few so-called Liberals who had been disappointed in securing office. The mock marriage of these incongruous elements begot the contempt and scorn of the Nation and suffered an ignominious defeat.

During this campaign—I think the first week in August—I had an occasion to test the imperial bluff of Conkling and the firm friendship of Grant. At this time I was connected with the Internal Revenue Department of the Government, with headquarters at St. Louis.

The supervising officers of the internal revenue had been cut down by law from twenty-five to ten, commencing July 1, 1872. There was a great political and personal scramble as to who should be retained. The supervisor for the district of Missouri, comprising five Western States, to the astonishment of his political friends, was superseded by a man from North Carolina. I was at the time up to my neck in politics and desired that the official status in Missouri should be continued, at least until after the election in November. To this end I secured urgent letters to General Grant from ex-Senator John B. Henderson, Henry T. Blow, and Chester H. Krum, the United States district attorney. I started immediately for Washington to see the President, but when I arrived I found that he had a few days before gone with a select party to the Thousand Islands and would stop for a few days at Utica to visit Mr. Conkling.

Before leaving Washington I called on General Babcock, the President's secretary, at the White House, on Internal Revenue Commissioner Douglass, and Mr. Boutwell, the Secretary of the Treasury, to see if the supervisor for the Missouri district could not be reinstated; but received no encouragement. In fact, the Secretary told me that the displacement of the supervisor was irrevocable. That August evening I took the fast train for New York and Utica, arriving at the latter place the same day President Grant visited Mr. Conkling. About 9 o'clock the next morning I strolled from Baggs' Hotel up Gennessee street to the mansion of the Senator. I was ushered into the parlor by a servant, sent my card to President Grant, and after waiting about ten minutes General Horace Porter, the President's private secretary, put in an appearance, greeted me cordially, took a seat and said that the President and family had not come down to breakfast, but if I had any communication to make he would convey it, saying at the same time that immediately after breakfast the President and party, with Mr. Conkling, Governor Seymour, and friends were to take a coaching trip to Trenton Falls, and in the evening there was to be a grand reception at Senator Conkling's home for the people of Utica. He also said that it would be impossible to see the President on any official business. I intimated to General Porter that I wished to see the President relative to the recent change in the supervisor's office. I could see from his countenance that he knew all about the matter and was doing the diplomatic to keep me from communicating in person with General Grant. However, I never yet consented to take a bluff from doorkeepers, ante-room agents, or private secretaries of men in public power, always making it a point to see and consult with the head, instead of hanging around the heels of lordly subordinates, who imagine that they carry the heart and conscience of their superiors in the hollow of their head and hand!

Bowing myself out of Mr. Conkling's parlor, I went back to Baggs' Hotel, determined to wait until the Presidential party returned that evening, and make another trial to see General Grant and present the three letters I had from his intimate friends in St. Louis.

With converging streams of people, at twilight, I took my way to the spacious grounds and mansion of Mr. Conkling, grandly illuminated by Chinese lanterns and decorated with flags and bunting in honor of the Chief Magistrate of the Nation. I arrived at the front steps just as the two coaches of the Presidential party drew up to deliver the guests, about a dozen people. A squad of police were present to keep the crowd from pressing on the noted visitors. The whole party passed up the steps, with Mr. Conkling bringing up the rear. I followed immediately after, the officer on guard, no doubt, thinking I was one of the guests. The ladies went into the broad hall, turned to the left to lay off their wraps, and the gentlemen filed to the right with General Grant in the lead.

Just as I was about to cross the threshold Senator Conkling turned about, and drawing himself up with an air that would have done Chesterfield and Cardinal Richelieu great credit, exclaimed: "Ah, Colonel, how are you?" "Very well, Senator," I replied. "Colonel, the President is to receive the people of Utica in an hour or so. I trust he may not be bothered with any official matters, as he is on a summer jaunt for health and pleasure."

"Senator, I have come more than a thousand miles to see the President, and have three important letters from his intimate friends in St. Louis to deliver to him in person. I trust you may permit me, at least, to pay my respects to the President of the United States while receiving the hospitality of yourself and friends, and I shall not refer to any official business unless the General first speaks of it himself."

"Ah, well, walk in, sir!" I passed into the double parlor, when Mr. Conkling disappeared, and soon after the President came forward, shook hands, bade me "good evening," and at once said: "Colonel, regarding that supervisor matter, I tried to retain your friend, but the pressure was so great that the Secretary of the Treasury had to put Cobb or Emory in his place."

"General, I promised Senator Conkling that I would not mention any official matter to you unless you spoke of it first. Now, here are three letters from your personal friends in St. Louis that I wish you would read, after which I'll be satisfied at your conclusion." He walked into the library, sat down at a desk, and read the letters. That of District Attorney Krum he read carefully, turned it over, and on the back of the same in his own handwriting ordered Secretary Boutwell to reinstate my political and official friend. The letter and indorsement are in existence today, a convincing proof to all that one should never be turned aside by subordinate difficulties, but press on to the fountain-head until absolute defeat or victory prevails.

I bade the General goodbye, shook hands, and took my departure for Washington, saw the Secretary, and carried back to the West the commission of the supervisor.

An incident showing the testy integrity of Senator Conkling came under my personal notice in the winter of 1874. Dropping into Willard's one evening to view the passing throng, I encountered Judge G., of Kentucky, who had a pending war claim of

$100,000 that had been shuttlecocked about for several years. It had passed the House of Representatives and was hanging fire on the Senate Calendar. Judge G., who had been my boyhood friend before the war, in Kentucky, asked me to introduce him to the New York Senator, saying that if he would make a short speech when the claim was called up, payment of his just debt for material furnished the Government would be speedily secured.

I consented reluctantly to introduce him to Mr. Conkling, knowing his abhorrence against the promiscuous war claims that were constantly coming up from the South. I told the old Judge on our way to the Senator's rooms that the New York statesman was a very proud and peculiar man, with the highest sense of personal honor, and that he must be handled very gingerly and convinced that the claim was thoroughly honest, else our mission would be a failure. Arriving at our destination, we were ushered into a parlor with bed-room in the rear, and I expressed the desire to see the Senator, giving my name and that of the Judge to the servant. The Senator soon appeared. I introduced Judge G., and all took seats, Mr. Conkling at his writing desk. The usual compliments of the evening were passed, and after a brief pause Judge G., a fine old confidential Kentuckian of the Bardwell Slote type, related his trials and tribulations, expense, and worry in trying to have the Government pay for horses, mules, cattle, forage, and wood that had been taken from him during the war, saying that the claim was then on the Senate Calendar, and if the Senator would speak but a few words in its favor he felt success would be certain, rounding up his remarks with the offer that if the Senator would do this he would pay him as a lawyer a fee of $10,000! If you had hit Conkling with a brick-bat between the eyes I don't think it would have flushed his face or stunned his body more than the last words of the Judge.

"Sir," said Conkling, standing to his full height, "an honest claim that needs a ten-thousand-dollar lawyer to secure its passage through Congress must be a very bad one! I am busy now! You will excuse me! Good evening!"

The old Judge arose, staggered from the room pale as a Peerless potato, and I felt as if a section of a brick house had fallen on my devoted head. We soon found ourselves on the pavement, and after walking a block in silence I broke the strain by saying, "Judge, you have ruined your case. You might as well pack up your grip and wander back to your blue grass farm in Bourbon. While Conkling is in Congress you will never get that claim through." "Well, John, I always had a kind of notion that I was a d—n fool, but now I know it. Let us go and get a drink of Old Bourbon, and I will then take the first train for ' Old Kaintuck ' and see the old woman and the girls once more before I die!"

A few days after this episode I was in the Marble Room of the Senate waiting for one of the Solons, when who should appear with his lordly stride but Conkling. We shook hands. He said: "Ah, Colonel, what is that gentleman's name that you introduced to me the other night?" I repeated his name, the Senator wrote it down on a card, made a dignified bow, and passed on to an alcove by the window, where a stately lady, the daughter of a former governor awaited his presence.

That $100,000 claim is still pending in Congress, and the poverty-stricken heirs are yet trying to get paid for material furnished the Government by their broken-hearted father, who ruined an honest case by slopping over with his tongue!

It is not generally known that Roscoe Conkling was a poet, perhaps not in the rhythmic sense, but in that lofty soaring of the soul above the sordid creatures of the vulgar valley, who wriggle out their little day and then sink beneath the clods they cultivate. He was no stickler for creeds, but measured mankind for their energy, loyalty, and truth. Life and death he viewed with philosophic composure and felt in his imperial nature the promptings of an eternal Omnipotence. From boyhood he memorized the rarest gems of prose and poetic literature, and in many of his forensic triumphs we may trace the pathetic or patriotic ideals of illustrious orators and poets. His mind was imbued with what it fed upon, and the intensity of his thought and manner inspired the listener with spontaneous rapture.

In the spring of 1880 I called at the rooms of Mr. Conkling with Dr. Elwood E. Thorne, Past Grand Master of Masons of New York, who wished to talk with his Senator upon the pending question of a protective tariff for sugar, the Doctor being an attorney for the sugar syndicate.

Just at the hour when twilight merges into night and stars and planets peep from out their mysterious realm, we were ushered into the presence of the Senator. We sat near the window, looking out on Fifteenth street at the hurrying throng wending their way to home, love, or despair. The Senator coincided with Thorne on the general principle of protection, but was desirous that sugar should be made as cheap as possible for the benefit of the poor, saying that the necessaries of life should be cheapened to the lowest possible point, while the luxuries, such as wines, liquors, malts, tobaccos, silks, satins, velvets, and jewels should bear the highest taxes and be paid by those who indulge their taste in these commodities.

At this moment in the Senator's argument flashes of lightning and rumbling thunder, accompanied by whistling wind and rattling rain, shook the building and caused Thorne and myself to pitch back from the window at the sudden outburst of the storm. Conkling kept his position like a rock, gazing at the scene with looks of admiration, like another Ajax on the heights of Olympus defying the lightning. Before we had time to make any remark on the sudden outburst of nature, he deliberately arose, struck a theatrical attitude, waved his right hand, and exclaimed in sonorous tones:

> "God moves in a mysterious way
> His wonders to perform,
> He plants His footsteps in the sea
> And rides upon the storm!"

And then, to exemplify the littleness of life and the evanescent joys of mortal midgets, he exclaimed:

> "Life is a dew drop, pendant on a flower;
> A sunbeam, glinting o'er a string of pearls;
> A vision of the future dimly seen;
> A little snowflake on a turbid stream;
> A maddening rush o'er a dread cataract,
> An atom borne on the breeze of time,
> Pinioned with hope for immortality!"

Thorne and myself clapped our hands with impulsive enthusiasm, forgetting the storm without while under the magic spell and poetic flights of the eloquent Senator.

Roscoe Conkling was a master of alliteration, euphony, synthesis, and repartee. More monosyllables are found in his orations, for their length, than in those of any American orator. His verbs and nouns were short, his adjectives and adverbs caustic, and his conjunctions scarce. He sent his thought through the mind of the listener swift as an arrow from the quiver of Diana. Diction was his delight, poetry his pleasure, and right his religion.

Today the bronze statues of Roscoe Conkling and his famous friend, William H. Seward, adorn the walks of Madison Square, and so long as streams of people from domestic or foreign lands shall roll up or down Broadway or the rocky foundation of Manhattan Island shall endure, so long shall the memory of these illustrious Americans shine out with Liberty enlightening the world by her beauty on the bounding bay.

> Their names shall live when marble, bronze, and bust
> Have crumbled into cold and silent dust,
> And Freedom, with her longest, latest breath,
> Shall sing their glory o'er a deathless death!

CHAPTER VIII.

GEN. F. E. SPINNER.

ELLICOTT, the sculptor, has finished the life-sized statue of Gen. F. E. Spinner, late Treasurer of the United States. It is cast in bronze and soon it will appear in front of the Treasury Department.

The statue is heroic, standing to the observer six feet, with a broad-brimmed hat, a corrugated brow, a crumpled cloak, wrinkled pants, firm foot and boot; and altogether, the best civilian statue in the District of Columbia.

It is well and just that the people of the United States should remember the cashier of the Republic.

Gen. Francis Elias Spinner, late Treasurer of the United States, was born in the town of Mohawk, Herkimer County, N. Y., January 21, 1802. His father, Peter, was born in Baden, Germany, January 18, 1768, emigrated to the United States in 1801, and died May 27, 1848, while minister of the Lutheran Church at Herkimer, eighty years of age. Like Luther, the elder Spinner had been a Catholic priest, but became a Protestant. He married a devotee of a nunnery and soon after came to the great Republic, where he continued his sacerdotal vocation until his death.

The son, Francis, was noted in his youth for pugnacity, generosity, and blunt honesty, characteristics that never forsook him. At an early age he was apprenticed to a confectioner, and afterward to a saddler, learning these trades to a partial degree, but soon his restless spirit longed for the excitement of political life, when he was appointed deputy sheriff and afterward elected sheriff of his county.

He was also major general of the New York State militia, and became cashier and president of a commercial bank. For four years he was deputy naval officer of the port of New York, and in 1854 he was elected to Congress as an anti-slavery Democrat, and after the Republican party was formed he represented that organization in Congress until the 3d of March, 1861, when he was requested by Secretary Chase and President Lincoln to become Treasurer of the United States, which position he held for fourteen years.

During the four years of the rebellion there was not an officer of the civil service of the Government that performed more active or important work than General Spinner. His strange and celebrated signature, first written on the printed sheets of greenbacks, was universally commented upon, and to the ordinary citizen who held the notes the name of the Treasurer was a puzzle. He adopted this cramped and peculiar signature, however, as he told me, for the purpose of foiling counterfeiters and making it difficult to imitate the original.

During the rapid and accumulating events of the spring, summer, and fall of 1861 and 1862 the greenback printing presses of the Government were run to their utmost limit to provide the sinews of war for the Army and Navy, and Spinner himself often remained at his desk more than twenty hours at a stretch signing and sending out the paper bullets that conquered the rebellion.

The desire of many Government clerks to enlist in the Army and Navy and battle for their country almost depleted some of the bureaus of their working force, and the Treasurer's office was no exception to the rule. To substitute the men General Spinner naturally thought of the employment of women, knowing that their deft fingers and rapid intuition could compete with, if not surpass, men as correct counters of new or old money.

General Spinner always felt a natural and commendable pride in first giving women an opportunity to make their own living by Government employment. Hundreds of mothers, wives, daughters, and sisters employed today in the various bureaus of the Government may well thank "the old watch-dog of the

Treasury" for his persistent and faithful adhesion to their interest; and each woman now in office should place a leaf, in the shape of a five-dollar bill, in the laurel wreath that will soon crown his bronze statue in front of the Treasury Department.

I was intimate with General Spinner and corresponded with him up to the time of his death, at Jacksonville, Fla., in January, 1891. In the summer of 1886 a discussion broke out in the newspapers as to who should get the credit for first recommending women as Government employees and afterward clerks. Some friends of Secretary Chase claimed the honor for him, but the weight of the witnesses and the actual records proved beyond a doubt that Spinner was the real pioneer that blazed the way for women to work in official capacity.

At the time General Spinner was summering at Pablo Beach, a seaside resort near Jacksonville, I wrote him regarding the discussion and with some acrimony against those who were trying to filch from him the glory of having first recommended the fair sex for Government labor. I have now before me a four-page autograph letter, dated August 4, 1886, at Pablo Beach, when he was eighty-four years of age; and in which occur these phrases relating to his employment of women: " The records of the Treasury Department will show that I am right in every case and my critics wrong. All the appointments of women that are claimed to have been made prior to the 9th of October, 1862, were made on my nomination for places in my then office, United States Treasurer. My records and the pay-rolls prove this. And then there are living witnesses in the persons of some of those mentioned still in Washington, one of them Miss Keller." This lady is still in office, as well as Miss Libbie Stoner, one of the first women employed in the Treasury Department.

General Spinner was a remarkable man in personal appearance, and one who attracted attention whenever seen. He stood nearly six feet tall, a round, broad, high forehead, slightly bald, with a corrugated countenance, thick, overhanging brows, shading a pair of deep-set grayish blue eyes that looked keenly into the motives of men. His voice was full and sonorous, his talk witty and direct, and when he was surrounded by social friends he was the most companionable of men, and was particularly polite and caressing to the fair sex, who were ever flattered by his attention.

He was a prime favorite with Congressmen, and when a Senator or Representative during the war and after could not find a snug place for his trusted constituent in the Departments, Spinner could generally be depended upon to furnish an asylum to the friends of his favorite and influential lawmakers. His official reports, estimates, and requests were always seconded by Chase and Lincoln, and when they came before the Ways and Means and Finance Committees they passed muster like a crack regiment on dress parade.

During the impeachment trial of President Andrew Johnson, in the fall of 1868, excitement ran very high in the various Departments of the Government among the clerks and their superior officers. The executive and legislative branches of the Government were arrayed against each other like forest stags at bay, and fighting over the Southern reconstruction laws and various Presidential vetoes with a vengeance that I have seldom seen in political life. "Johnson clubs" were formed in the Departments by subservient policy clerks, who are always found to "crook the pregnant hinges of the knee that thrift might follow fawning." Most officials took sides for or against impeachment, and "spotters" could be found in every office to report those who clung to Congress and favored the official decapitation of the President. Spinner was one of the few Government officers that did not favor or cringe to the dictates of "my policy," and while the impeachment proceedings and excitement incident thereto were at the highest pitch he wrote a personal letter to a Congressional friend severely condemning President Johnson and his associates, respectful, of course, but firm as his own sterling character.

During my official residence, in the revenue service, at St.

Louis, from 1870 to 1875, I corresponded with the General, often sending him some of my newspaper articles, soldier orations, and social speeches, and he never failed to reply in the heartiest manner.

In 1875 a contest arose between General Spinner and Secretary Bristow over some appointments the Secretary of the Treasury wanted to make against the will and over the head of the Treasurer. All former Secretaries of the Treasury had never interfered with the appointments made in the Treasurer's office, as it was regarded as a great national bank, the Treasurer giving a personal bond for $100,000 for the proper care and account of the money of the Republic. It was by common consent admitted that as the Treasurer was responsible for the cash, he should be allowed to select his own counters and cashiers, but Bristow sought to thrust some of his political friends into Spinner's office. The General kicked, and the matter was brought to the notice of President Grant by Bristow. Spinner said that he would resign unless he was allowed to select the working tools of his office, and Bristow insisted that he was the appointing power under the law and would have his own way or vacate the Treasury Department.

Grant, being schooled as a disciplinarian and influenced by some personal and political friends, sided at the time with the Secretary of the Treasury, and Spinner at once resigned the office that he had held so long with rare honor to himself and great profit to his country. In a few months Grant was forced to dismiss Bristow, who brought upon his head the scandal of "the whisky ring," that made such a noise in its day.

The spring before the General retired from office he visited his family in Florida for a short vacation from his arduous labors as Treasurer, and on his return to the Capital he came back by the way of New Orleans, up the Mississippi River, by one of the palace steamboats that then plied between the Crescent City and St. Louis, and stopped off a few days to see some of his subordinate officers and view the sights and growing greatness of the metropolis that aspired to be the future Capital of the Republic.

The most prominent people of St. Louis called on him at the Planters' House, where I was then boarding with my family, and vied with each other in showing respect and attention to the great war Treasurer of the United States. One pleasant, sunny afternoon I invited himself, his daughter and adopted daughter to take a carriage drive and see the sights of the Mound City.

In the course of the drive we visited the celebrated Shaw's garden, one of the rarest botanical gardens in the United States.

The General and his daughter alighted at the lodge gate, and we proceeded to the summer home of Henry Shaw, located at one end of the garden, amid rare trees, shrubs, vines, and ferns, and beautiful flowers growing in grace and exhaling perfume on the wings of the gentle zephyrs that blew over this earthly paradise.

We sent in our cards, and were ushered into the reception room. Soon afterward the sage of the flowers appeared in a silk skull cap. Mr. Shaw produced a register of visitors and asked the General to give him his celebrated signature, saying, laughingly, that some future wanderers might have a fine time among his pet flowers, and working out his signature as an autographic puzzle. The General replied: "Mr. Shaw, I think it has puzzled some of the counterfeiters, and it puzzles a great many other people as to how to secure enough of the 'greenbacks' with my cramped chirography." We all signed our names, the General, I think, composing a phrase before his signature. Mr. Shaw then escorted us through the grounds, explaining, as he went, the names, virtues, and peculiarities of his botanical beauties, growing in regular beds outdoors or blooming in pots in the long green-houses. I remember one plant about three feet high that he took great interest in. I think he called it a breathing or pulse plant, and that it had come from the Amazon, in South America. Its small branches and slender leaves moved up and down with the rhythmic action of heart beats, and it seemed to be a living object. We stood in amazement at the sight of this rare plant, and General Spinner asked Mr. Shaw if he thought it had a heart and soul. The octogenarian replied: "I am as certain as I live that the same Supreme Being that called us into life and breathed into us His celestial spirit reigns in this wonderful plant and teaches us the lesson of immortality!"

We passed on, and, going back to the house at his pressing invitation, we lingered at the tomb that he had prepared to encase his mortal remains when life's fitful fever was over. "General," he said, pointing to the marble sarcophagus, "there is where I expect to rest when the sun shall shine for me no more, and since I will not be able to attend to my lovely flowers with hands of flesh, my spirit can watch over them daily and nightly, and their own beauty will induce those to whom I have bequeathed them to watch with jealous care for their preservation." We were deeply impressed by the solemn language and surrounding scene, a man standing beside his own tomb delivering his own funeral oration. When we arrived at the house we found a light lunch prepared, and the old sage pressed us to partake, producing some fine old sherry wine, clear as amber and seemingly as old as himself. In a short time we finished, and, as General Spinner wished to take the train that night for Washington, hurried away, bidding Mr. Shaw and his beautiful garden a fond farewell, he not forgetting, however, to present each of the ladies with a beautiful bouquet and the General and myself with a single jacqueminot to wear as a boutonniere.

In due course we arrived at the Planters' House. The General and his daughters were much pleased with their entertainment by Mr. Shaw, and to the day of their death, no doubt, remembered with pleasure the St. Louis botanist.

The last time I saw General Spinner was at Willard's Hotel, on his way to Florida, two years before his death. The ravages of a cancer had greatly disfigured his face and a settled gloom seemed to have taken possession of his countenance, while his natural irritability was increased. He saw but few persons, and those some of the true and faithful clerks that had honestly served him while Treasurer. The morning I called was dark and rainy. He was located on the second floor on the corner near the F-street entrance. When I put in an appearance at his parlor room he rose with some effort, saluted me kindly, and I remarked, "Why, General, how well you look." He impulsively replied, "Now, look here, Joyce, you know that's a lie!" I made some explanatory remarks and turned the conversation into another channel, knowing, of course, that my first salutation was not exactly the truth, but uttered as the usual compliment among friends. But I'll never forget the sterling sincerity of Spinner, who would not accept a passing social compliment when he felt it to be false!

The waters of the romantic Mohawk now murmur a requiem to his memory, and the rolling hills and blooming vales that blessed his boyhood will long echo the praises of this illustrious man, who handled $3,000,000,000 during the civil war and accounted for every cent to a grateful people, who will always cherish his memory while truth, loyalty, and honesty reign in the human heart!

> He stands in bronze without a peer or clan—
> The bold, heroic figure of a man,
> To tell to generations yet unborn
> That he was one who held up to all scorn
> The man or woman who would not do right
> And on great Virtue draw a draft at sight.
> He'll stand for truth along the columned years,
> And bring to patriot eyes pathetic tears,
> That one so good and great should pass away
> And mingle with the cold, unconscious clay.
> But what he did in life will shine and grow
> Like waters from the hills that flash and flow,
> To gather greater volume as they run
> And scatter blessings from each sun to sun.
> To woman in her struggle to be free

He gave his hand and heart right royally,
And battled for her rights both night and day
To have a chance to work and get her pay.
No pelf or power could sway him to the wrong,
He stood like granite crags, so bold and strong—
That all the storms of life could not deface
A character—the finest of his race!
In legislative halls he stood ornate,
With pivot points and truth to close debate,
And flashed his sabre in the face of greed,
A gallant charger who was born to lead!
As cashier of a nation, grand and great,
He stood a splendid pillar of the State;
Disbursing billions with an honest hand
To save the glory of his native land.
His name shall brighten as the years prolong
The words of wisdom and the soul of song,
And while a woman lives to love and pray,
His glory shall be sounded to the latest day—
Teaching the world that equal rights for all
Shall triumph round this grand terrestrial ball.
Here let him stand through summer suns or frost,
To tell a Nation that no good is lost—
For doing duty like the lordly man,
Who sometimes thinks that in this earthly plan
The Great Creator only counts the male,
And woman but a fancy thing to hail!
This statue that we dedicate today
Will stand when granite columns melt away,
And tell to tottering age and blooming youth
That Glory centers in immortal Truth,
That man reveres the honest, patriot heart
Who struggles nobly and performs his part—
In all the walks of life, through weal or woe,
A faithful friend and an outspoken foe.
He cringed not to the power of wealth or state;
He only knew that to be true was to be great,
And did his duty, firm and square and kind—
The honest output of a heart and mind.
He fawned not to the rabble howl or cheers
In all his life, near ninety glorious years,
But kept his soul as pure and true and bright

As stars that glitter in an Arctic night.
And he who does his duty shall be blessed
When angel voices call him home to rest,
Where Heavenly choirs chant their matin hymns,
And golden goblets filled up to the brims,
With living wine, to cheer the noble soul
That fights for right to an eternal goal.
Glory to Spinner and his loyal band
Who kept us still a brave, united land,
From where the fair magnolia tree doth shine
To golden sands replete with fruit and wine.
And as the ages wing their flight away
We'll sound in chorus a grand deathless lay
For Liberty and Truth against the world:
Our glorious banner still to man unfurled—
An emblem of the brave, the pure, and free,
The rainbow colors of eternity!

CHAPTER IX.

SAMUEL SULLIVAN COX.

SAMUEL SULLIVAN COX, familiarly known as "Sunset," was of Irish lineage and was born in Zanesville, Ohio, on the 30th of September, 1824, and died in the city of New York on the 10th of September, 1889. His grandfather, from New Jersey, was a general in the Revolutionary War and served under Washington in many of the battles that established our Republic and drove monarchy from our shores.

Mr. Cox graduated in the classics at Brown College, and in the spring of 1853 became editor of the Ohio *Statesman*, published at Columbus. It was while managing this journal that he derived the sobriquet of "Sunset," which arose out of an eloquent editorial description of a sunset that flashed over Columbus on the afternoon of the 8th of May, 1853.

It is well worth preserving in enduring form as a brilliant specimen of word painting rarely surpassed by any writer. Here it is:

A GREAT OLD SUNSET.

"What a stormful sunset was that of last night!

"How glorious the storm and how splendid the setting sun. We do not remember to have ever seen the like on our round globe. The scene opened in the west with the whole horizon full of golden interpenetrating luster, which colored the foliage and brightened every object into its own rich dyes.

"The colors grew deeper and richer until the golden luster was transfused into a storm cloud full of brightest lightning, which leaped in dazzling zigzags all around and over the city. The wind arose with fury, the slender shrubs and giant trees made obeisance to its majesty. Some even snapped before its face.

"The strawberry beds and grape plots turned up their blooms to see Zepyhrus march by. As the rains came and the pools formed, there appeared in the azure belt a celestial city. It became more vivid, revealing strange forms and peerless fanes, rare and grand in this mundane sphere.

"But the cloud and sun-capped city vanished only to give place to a magic isle, where the most beautiful forms of foliage appeared, imaging a paradise in the distance and a purified celestial air.

"The sun, wearied of the elemental commotion, sank behind the green plains of the West. The great eye in Heaven, however, went not down without a dark brow hanging over its departing light. The rich flush of the unearthly light had passed away and the rain had ceased, when the solemn church bells pealed, the laughter of children resounded—joy, after the storm is over, the carol of flitting birds, while the forked and purple weapon of the skies still darted illumination around the Starling College, trying to rive its rugged angles and leap into its dark windows.

"Candles are lighted. The piano strikes up its melodious strains. We feel it is good to have a home; good to be on the earth, where such revelations of beauty and power may be made.

"And, as we cannot refrain from reminding our readers of everything wonderful in our city, we have begun and ended our impulsive etching of a sunset, which comes so rarely that its resplendent glory should be committed to immortal type!"

I was introduced to "Sunset" Cox in the winter of 1869 by Hon. Charles A. Eldredge, a leader of the House of Representatives from Wisconsin. Cox had just been elected from New York City to Congress, having served four previous terms from Ohio. He was in the prime of life, vigorous, alert, bright, witty, and generous to a fault.

While a Democrat of unfaltering fealty, he during the whole civil war held up the hands of the Government and voted men and money for the suppression of the rebellion. He was the author of one of our best census and apportionment enactments.

But, what will carry his name and fame down the years is the establishment of the Life-saving Service and the propulsion he gave to the letter-carrier system of the Nation. He was the constant guardian of the ocean life savers and letter carriers, two of the most important branches of the Government, which merits the sympathy and encomiums of the people. Great danger is constantly incurred by the ocean life savers, and the most withering exposure is often endured uncomplainingly by the faithful and honest letter carriers.

I have often heard "Sunset" Cox express these sentiments around the social board, and in the halls of Congress, only in a more emphatic form.

He was the life and joy of the social board, bubbling with wit and humor as bright as the sparkling jewels that race around the rim of the wine cup.

I shall never forget the 22d day of February, 1881. Passing down Pennsylvania avenue about 10 o'clock in the morning with Hon. Charles A. Eldredge, when the city wore its holiday garb in celebration of the Father of his Country, nearing the National Theater, we came in contact with "Sunset" Cox, General Belknap, Colonel Crosby, and John Albaugh, the noted actor and theatrical manager. Cox seemed to be full of the glorious day and asked us to "celebrate." We unanimously accepted his invitation, and proceeded to a private room in the theatre. Wine was ordered, and distributed by John Hartnett, a son of the Emerald Isle, who had lost none of his wit in crossing the ocean.

I moved that the "House" elect a "Speaker" of the social conclave, and at the same time nominated "Sunset" Cox. John Albaugh seconded the motion, and it was carried without a dissenting vote. We demanded a speech or a song, when the "Speaker" launched out into eloquence and poetry. Holding up his glass to the Hibernian Hebe, he sang:

Fill the goblet again! for I never before
Felt the glow which now gladdens my heart to its core;
Let us drink!—who will not?—since through life's varied round
In the goblet alone no deception is found!

I have tried in its turn all that life can supply;
I have basked in the beam of a dark rolling eye,
I have loved!—who has not?—but what heart can declare,
That pleasure existed while passion was there.

Long life to the grape! for when summer is flown,
The age of our nectar shall gladden our own;
We must die!—who shall not?—may our sins be forgiven—
And Hebe shall never be idle in Heaven!

We cheered to the echo and drank standing. I could imagine the spirit of the glorious Lord Byron listening to his social song, sung so sweetly by "Sunset" Cox. Like Oliver Twist, we called for more, and the genial "Sunset" gave us a fine dramatic rendition of Melnot's description of his palace on the Lake of Como, where he wished to harbor the beautiful Pauline in the magic meshes of his affection.

John Albaugh, by special request, rendered in his inimitable way a scene from Brutus and the immortal soliloquy of the melancholy Dane. General Belknap told some racy war stories. Mr. Eldredge told some laughable Congressional yarns. Colonel Crosby gave us the beef-contract story of the irrepressible Mark Twain, while I recited a few of my poems, sang a song, and whistled the mocking bird.

After an extended symposum we adjourned in due form, feeling satisfied that each patriot had done full justice to the birthday of the immortal Washington.

*   *   *   *   *

While Mr. Cox was minister to Turkey, in 1885, I had published in New York, by Thomas R. Knox & Co., a volume, entitled "Peculiar Poems," and in it had one "Lindalou" dedicated to my esteemed friend Cox. I sent him a copy of the book with my compliments.

Soon after I received from him a long letter from Constantinople containing some very funny and satirical remarks.

I picture "Lindalou" as the light of the harem and intimate that "Sunset" is in love with her, making him say in one verse—

> I live in the light of the harem,
> And bask 'neath her beautiful eyes.
> Recline on rich Ottoman velvets
> To gaze on the Bosphorus skies,
> Lindalou and her sweet paradise.

Here are a few sentences from his humorous letter: "I have read your 'Peculiar Poems' with great pleasure, but why should you hitch me up to a harem beauty and put me in the way of a divorce from Mrs. C. and have the Grand Vizier strangle an innocent 'Buckeye' and pitch him into the deep waters of the Golden Horn is more than I can understand; and that, you know, would lead to an instant war between the United States and the Ottoman Empire, which would in all human probability set the whole world up in arms, all on account of 'Lindalou,' a fairy-like form, moulded in beauty and grace, who floats like a sylph on the light wings of space.

"Joyce, you have ruined me! I am going to send in my resignation very soon to President Cleveland, who can appreciate my 'Lindalou' situation, for I know that if the Sultan gets on to this 'light of the harem' business I'm a 'goner.'

"I'd rather be back anyhow with the Tigers of Tammany and the 'boys' of Washington than to risk my life monkeying around 'Lindalou.'"

Mr. Cox was at one time Speaker *pro tem.* of the House of Representatives, and I have often heard his keen, ready wit on the floor and his fair and impartial rulings in the chair. His wit may have at times interfered with the dignity of his public positions and kept him from higher stations, where silent and solemn mediocrity often reach, by a system of somber philosophy, but his genial humor kept him in tone with the masses, and to this day they revere his memory. He was an extensive traveler, having circled the globe and gathered golden treasures of thought wherever he wandered. He was the author of several interesting books, among them "Arctic Sunbeams," " Orient Sunbeams," " Why We Laugh," etc.

His Congressional, campaign, and miscellaneous orations were masterpieces of wit, humor, and philosophy, seldom leaving a sting in the minds of the hearers, but, on the contrary, a grace and pleasure such as Pericles might bestow on an Athenian audience.

The exit of such a genial and generous being from the ranks of mankind leaves a broken link in the chain of affection, and the world feels lonelier for the absence of a man who lived but to love and gave his best thought and action for the elevation and progress of his race.

> While love and truth are ever grand,
> And noble deeds prevail,
> The name of " Sunset " Cox shall stand
> Through every ocean gale.

As an evidence of the esteem and affection in which " Sunset " Cox was held by his colleagues and compeers it is only necessary for the reader to glance at the following epigrammatic and eloquent tributes paid to the illustrious dead, when his funeral obsoquies were held in the Congress of the United States.

The genial and witty Amos Cummings, of New York, says :

He aided in reconciling the sections, he shielded the Israelite from political debarkation, he shortened the tramp of the weary postman, he made the angry waves jubilant with the song of rescue. He was a star in our political galaxy from which men take observations. Whatever weakness he had came not from the poverty, but from the plenitude of his power, and when occasion demanded he buried his political animosities in his patriotism.

The pugnacious, industrious, and classic Benton McMillin, of Tennessee, says:

Cox was a great student. When Atticus asked Cicero to recount the means by which he had achieved his marvelous success, the orator replied that he studied three years for the forum and practiced two years, during which he met Hortensius; that he was not satisfied with his own style, and that he traveled two years in the East to study and reform it; that during this entire seven years he hardly let a day escape him that he did not write something, memorize something, and compose something. Mr. Cox, like the eloquent Tully, was an untiring worker. I knew no man who could work more rapidly or did work more constantly. He was gifted with rare ability to conceive beautiful and forcible thoughts and extraordinary eloquence to promulgate them.

He loved his country with the fervor which should characterize a patriot whose ancestors had fought in the Revolution.

General Grosvenor, of Ohio, remarks:

The bright things which he said and which have passed into permanent record were spontaneous and not prearranged. His wit was born at the moment. His repartee came rushing forth, suggested by his opponent. The very challenge produced the answer. The thought came as a flash of lightning. It was inspiration.

He was a man without malice. He fought hard and dealt heavy blows in a contest, but when the battle ceased there was no bitterness behind. He had statesmanship as well as politics.

Mr. Frank Lawler, of Illinois, an Irish patriot, says of Cox:

He was a representative American, proud of his country, proud of the American people, and devoted to the ennoblement of the American Republic. His sympathies were broad and acute. They welled out to all humanity wherever there was suffering and affliction among the people.

Mr. McAdoo, of New Jersey, an eloquent son from the Emeral Isle and an American to the backbone, says:

Gifted, versatile, cosmopolitan, the range of his mental vision sped from land to land and ranged the orbits of other worlds in star-gemmed space. Intensely American in the best and highest sense, he was neighbor and brother to all mankind. He lived in close communion with nature, loving the beautiful and the good, and his pulses timed their beat with the throbs of the great heart of humanity, and his very heart-strings vibrated to the sublime anthem of universal liberty.

Mr. Covert, of New York, pays an eloquent tribute to our

departed friend, and quotes the beautiful and solemn poem of Gen. Albert Pike, the great luminary of Masonry.

And so, loving and loved, Cox passed from the semi-darkness of this life into the eternal light and glory of the light hereafter.

> " To the past go more dead faces
>   Every year,
> As the loved leave vacant places
>   Every year.
> Everywhere their sad eyes meet us;
> In the evening's dusk they greet us,
> And to come to them entreat us
>   Every year.
>
> " You are growing old, they tell us,
>   Every year;
> You are more alone, they tell us,
>   Every year.
> You can win no new affection;
> You have only recollection,
> Deeper sorrow and dejection
>   Every year.
>
> " But the truer life draws nigher
>   Every year,
> And its morning star climbs higher
>   Every year.
> Earth's hold on us grows slighter,
> And its heavy burden lighter,
> And the dawn immortal brighter
>   Every year."

The witty and epigrammatic Ash. Caruth, of Kentucky, says:

Not only was Cox a great orator and a great statesman, but he was a scholar besides. I asked him once how he found time in his busy life to give attention to literary matters and charm by printed page as he had by spoken word, and he told me that God had given him a helpmate in the person of his wife, and that she had shared his labors as she had indeed doubled the pleasures of his life. And thus, loved at home, admired by his peers, honored by the people, the statesman, the wit, the scholar, passed his life away. The passing years left but little impress on his brow and made no mark upon his heart.

General Wheeler, of Alabama, a dashing cavalry officer of the late Confederacy, pays "Sunset" this noble and sententious compliment:

Firm as a rock, brilliant as a star, artless as a child, pure as a woman, God endowed him for a good purpose with a resiliency of wit, a faculty of impersonation, and an irresistible mimicry and a dramatic power that were inexhaustible. How much the world owes to such a nature we cannot tell. It is often a greater good to cause a laugh than to start a tear. We all cry enough, God knows, and have enough to cry about, and we need no impulse in that direction. But he who can scatter our gloom by innocent merriment has been to us an emancipator!

Senator Voorhees, of Indiana, a genuine gentleman and lofty orator, speaks of our dear friend in this heroic fashion:

With the eye of a philosopher and with a soul filled with the poetry and sublimity of high historic associations, he saw almighty Rome, climbed the Pyramids, and stood upon Mount Calvary. He traversed deserts on the camel's back and camped at nightfall with the Bedouin at long-sought wells of fresh water. He floated on the waters of the Nile, and plucked the lotus, the Egyptians' symbol of the creation. He marked the course of the Euphrates; looked upon the Red Sea where Pharaoh attempted to cross in pursuit of fugitive slaves; drank from the river Jordan, and slept by the cooling fountains of Damascus.

Wherever he traveled and in whatever clime he sojourned what a stanch and genuine American he was! The sunbeams of the Orient, the soft skies of Italy, the grandest scenery of the Alps, were not so attractive or sublime to him as the face of nature in his own western home. After gliding on the waters of the blue Danube and along the castellated heights of the Rhine, he was wont to say that the Hudson between Albany and New York and the Ohio from Steubenville to Cincinnati presented more beauty to the eye of the traveler than any other rivers of the world.

Sir, such a character as I have but imperfectly delineated must take and hold a front place in the history of his country. His works are durable contributions to the cause of human progress, and they cannot perish. Their influences will bide the test of time and will go on forever!

Senator Vest, of Missouri, the ever-ready and humorous statesman, says:

Cox was in some respects the most remarkable man I have known in public affairs. Whilst there was nothing majestic or rugged in his nature, he was beyond question better adapted to public life as known to the American people than any other man in all my acquaintance. He was capable of indefatigable labor, with varied accomplishments, versatile talents, wonderful eloquence, and a tenacity of purpose which knew nothing like failure.

Hon. J. Proctor Knott, of Kentucky, made a grand oration upon the memory of Mr. Cox at the great Cooper Union meeting in New York. Here are a couple of sparkling gems from his symmetrical masterpiece, and would do credit to Pericles, who delivered the eulogium over the dead Athenians:

Beneath the rippling, sparkling surface of his never-failing, effervescent humor there lay the serenest depths of thought, an energy of will that knew no impediment, and powers of intellectual labor that defied fatigue.

His hunger for information was as ravenous as the genius of famine. It devoured everything that could amuse the fancy, improve the mind, or elevate the soul. His fealty to the Union was paramount to all other obligations; his pride in its grandeur and power touched the extremest limit of exultant enthusiasm; his veneration for its Constitution was the supreme sentiment of his soul; his faith in its destiny transcended the wildest dream of optimism.

CHAPTER X.

GEORGE D. PRENTICE.

THE poet-journalist is sometimes found in the same person, but the Muse soars aloft and circles over the tripod like an Alpine eagle over the hungry vulture of the valley.

The true poet, profound or ethereal, is like a wandering spirit shot out of its celestial orb into a strange planet, where his soaring and sensitive nature wear out his weary wings battling against the sordid creatures that stare in amazement at the brilliant colors of his plumage.

Some day he is found dead in a little corner of the globe with his bright wings folded forever, his impulsive warm heart cold, and his classic face furrowed with the wrinkles of uncongenial elements that have left him a wreck on the shores of time.

Over the cold ashes of the poet the world will gather with mournful mien and sigh at the grave of buried genius. Yesterday, he suffered for sympathy and bread; today, a funeral train honors his memory; tomorrow, a monument will point posterity to a prodigy of celestial aspirations, whose songs will thrill the heart of mankind through the crowding ages.

> Yes; when he's seen no more in field or town,
>   And all his mortal part lies cold and dead,
> Some sage or city for their own renown
>   Will give a shaft where once he needed bread.

I have had the pleasure of meeting three of the most illustrious American poets—Henry W. Longfellow, from the pine-clad hills of Maine; William Cullen Bryant, from the granite hills of Massachusetts, and George D. Prentice, from the rolling rivers and circling bays of Connecticut. These famous men had many elements in common and have left their "footprints on the sands of time."

Longfellow was purely poetical, while Bryant and Prentice joined journalism with poetry, and through the press wrought in the interest of statesmanship and the success of republican government. They were profound scholars, and, while not endowed with the elemental philosophy of Aristotle, Plato, or Newton, their views of life, death, and time, as exemplified in the "Psalm of Life," "Thanatopsis," and "The Closing Year" will always remain masterpieces of literary philosophy.

Longfellow exclaimed with pathetic voice:

> "Art is long and Time is fleeting,
> And our hearts tho' stout and brave,
> Still like muffled drums are beating
> Funeral marches to the grave.
>
> " Trust no future, howe'er pleasant!
> Let the dead past bury its dead!
> Act, act in the living present!
> Heart within and God o'erhead!"

Bryant views death in this sublime flight:

> "The hills;
> Rock-ribbed and ancient as the sun, the vales
> Stretching in pensive quietness between;
> The venerable woods; rivers that move
> In majesty, and the complaining brooks
> That make the meadows green; and poured round all
> Old ocean's gray and melancholy waste—
> Are but the solemn decorations
> Of the great tomb of man!"

Prentice contemplates on Time and "The Closing Year" in these profound and philosophic phrases, superior in my estimation to anything ever written by his compeers—dished off, too, on the impulse of the moment at the clamorous solicitation of a lot of little newsboys, who wanted an address to sell to their patrons on New Year's Day.

"'Tis midnight's holy hour, and silence now
Is brooding like a gentle spirit o'er
The still and pulseless world.   *   *   *
The year has gone, and with it many a glorious throng
Of happy dreams. Its mark is on each brow,
Its shadow in each heart. In its awful course
It waved its scepter o'er the beautiful,
And they are not.   *   *   *
Remorseless time!
Fierce spirit of the glass and scythe,
What power can stay him in his silent course
Or melt his iron heart to pity.
On, still on, he presses and forever.   *   *   *
The proud bird—
The condor of the Andes that can soar
Through heaven's unfathomable depths, or brave
The fury of the northern hurricane
And bathe his plumage in the thunder's home—
Furls his broad wings at nightfall and sinks down
To rest upon his mountain crag—but Time
Knows not the weight of sleep or weariness.   *   *   *

"New empires rise—
Gathering the strength of hoary centuries,
And rush down like the Alpine avalanche,
Startling the nations; and the very stars,
Yon bright and burning blazonry of God,
Glitter awhile in their eternal depths,
And like the Pleaids, loveliest of their train,
Shoot from their glorious spheres and pass away
To darkle in the trackless void; yet Time,
Time, the tomb builder, holds his fierce career,
Dark, stern, all-pitiless, and pauses not
Amid the mighty wrecks that strew his path
To sit and muse, like other conquerors,
Upon the fearful ruin he has wrought!

Many of the personal poems of Prentice rank in the first class, notably his "Lines to an Absent Wife" and his "Name in the Sand," in which his soul soars up to his Creator.

"And yet, with Him who counts the sands
And holds the waters in his hands
I know a lasting record stands
Inscribed against my name;
Of all this mortal part has wrought
Of all my thinking soul has thought
And from these fleeting moments caught,
For glory or for shame!"

In the presence of Longfellow, seated in his library at Cambridge, with his snowy locks, benevolent face, and soothing voice the gentle spirit of Evangeline and Minnehaha seemed to hover near, and his melancholy wail, by the sea, at "the bridge" spontaneously bubbled up in my mind.

" How often, O, how often
I had wished that the ebbing tide
Would bear me away on its bosom
O'er the ocean wild and wide!"

It was the summer before the poet's death, in 1881, that I gazed for the last time on the sweet singer, and even then I could see that the "ebbing tide" was silently bearing him away o'er the celestial ocean that washes the shores of immortality!

I was in New York City in 1875 at the Astor House and expressed a desire to a literary friend to see the poet Bryant. He remarked that the poet did not come to the office of the *Post* very often, but we might step over and see Godwin and find out. We went and luckily found the literary lion, to whom I was introduced. He impressed me deeply, spoke in a solemn voice, looked like an Oriental sage, with a grand dome of thought, jutting brow and flowing beard, over a body not rugged or strong. I spoke of reading his "Thanatopsis" at school, in Kentucky, and of being infatuated with all the grand poets of the ages.

"Yes;" said he, "I'm glad you like poetry. It has been the heaven of my earthly career, and were I naked of all worldy trappings, I would not exchange the glorious pleasures of the Muses for all the wealth of Crœsus. 'Thanatopsis' was one of my earliest poems, and, strange to say, many of my literary friends throughout the world think it my best production."

Mr. Bryant, may I ask what you think about it?

"Well," said the sage, "it is hard to battle against the verdict of the world, but for a broad view of human life and teaching the truth of immortality I think "The Flood of Years" contains the best thoughts I have uttered; and yet some of my minor poems, expressing the grief of my surcharged heart over the 'Death of the Flowers' or the carnage of 'The Battlefield' have quatrains that may live when some of my more pretentious lines are buried in the grave of forgetfulness. For instance—

" Truth crushed to earth shall rise again;
The eternal years of God are hers;
But error, wounded, writhes in pain
And dies among his worshipers!'

The grand old patriarch paused, we arose, bade him a last farewell, and found our way into the tumbling, rumbling life that swells the tide of human affairs on Broadway.

I became personally acquainted with George D. Prentice, the celebrated wit, journalist, and poet in the month of January, 1863, at Louisville, Ky. He was then about sixty-one years of age, and the ravages of time had deeply furrowed his features and twisted his gnarled form. I was at the time about twenty-one years of age and adjutant of the Twenty-fourth Kentucky Regiment. My regiment was camped at the "Oaklands," a suburban site near the city. Previous to my enlistment I had from my home in Mount Sterling sent some fugitive verses to the Louisville *Journal* that appeared in the poet's corner, and, of course, like all young fledgling who aspire to court the Muses, I was flattered and imagined that the spirits of Homer, Byron, and Edgar Allen Poe were looking right down on my growing greatness. I felt, too, that the author of "The Closing Year" was cognizant of a new-found star in the celestial realm of poesy.

I concluded to call on the great Llama of literature and loyalty, and to this end secured a pass for forty-eight hours to protect me against the scrutinizing eyes of provost guards or the shoulder-strapped minions of Colonel Mark Mundy, the post commander.

I had been paid off and received some four months' back wages, purchased a stunning uniform with gold gilt buttons and staff shoulder-straps almost as large as a bar of soap! Thus, panoplied in all the trappings of glorious war, with a pocketful of cash, I sailed out of camp, as it were, in company with my schoolmate, Will. L. Visscher, passed over Broadway and into Green street, where the old *Journal* office was located. I imagined that the overcoat of General Grant would not make a vest for this proud adjutant, and that the ladies I passed on the street were gloriously impressed with my military bearing.

As a bracer to the ordeal I was about to undergo, I invited Visscher to join me in a bottle of wine at the celebrated Walker's Exchange. After irrigating our anatomy with the exhilarating fluid we proceeded to the *Journal* office. Visscher left me at the bottom of the steps leading to the editorial room of the great poet and journalist, saying that he had an engagement to meet one of the belles of Louisville, but promised that he would see me in an hour or two at the Galt House.

It was then about 3 o'clock in the afternoon. I marched up the rickety stairs around a dark hall filled with stacks of blank paper and was stalking on to the den of the editor when a "smoked Yankee," like an ogre, intercepted my further progress and exclaimed, "What ye want, sah?" I replied that I wished to see Mr. Prentice. "Send in yer cad, sah!" I had forgotten to lay in a supply of cards, but with that presence of mind that never forsakes a great soldier tore off a corner of the printing paper in the hall, wrote my name, and gave it to the imperial menial. He soon returned and waved me into the royal sanctum. I straightened up, shook down my trousers, settled into my coat as if moulded for the garment, and then marched in with the air of a drum major on dress parade. I looked around the shabby, naked room, saw a stout, low-built man writing away at a rude desk with a very tremulous hand. His head was large, round, and somewhat bald, but the bumps and furrows on his brow reminded me of Socrates or some of the ancient philosophers whose pictures I had seen in historical and classical works. He did not look up, although he must have known that I was present, for I coughed, tramped around, and becoming impatient at non-recognition finally threw on the floor a pile of newspapers off the only stool in the room, right near his desk, and planted my military greatness on the sight of the displaced literature. He went right on with his scratching hieroglyphics until he got to the bottom of the page, and threw down his pen, whirled about in his chair, and with a look of mingled madness and sententious satire said, "Who are you?" "I'm a fool!" "So am I; shake!" And that was our first acquaintance. His brow began to relax its intensity and a furtive smile came over his his countenance as he gazed on my military make-up.

"So you're an adjutant, are you? What's that?"

"That, sir," I replied, "is the hinge to the door jamb of a colonel."

"An, indeed; do you ever drink?"

"Never; except when alone or in company."

"Tom, my carriage!"

He took up his gold-headed cane, hobbled down the stairs to the street, where we took the carriage and rode to the Galt House. I was ushered into a wine room back of the office and introduced to Major Silas Miller, the proprietor, and to Mr. Magoffin and Mr. Owsley. Prentice put up two fingers and soon there appeared a servant with two quart bottles of Heidsieck wine. Five glasses were brought, and the waiter filled them to the brim. Prentice held up his glass and said: "Gentlemen, I want to drink to the health of our young adjutant, who tells me that he is a poet and a fool!" We drank with a vim, and, although I felt nettled at the toast, I thought myself too sharp to reply to these old, wise, and witty cronies, who spent part of most every afternoon in Bacchanalian revelry. Visscher appeared at this moment, and I introduced him to the quartet of solid citizens.

Another glass was brought, and we filled to the brim once more. I proposed the toast, "The United States." They drank it, although Magoffin and Owsley did not seem very enthusiastic about my patriotic sentiment.

I put up two fingers for the eye of the "contraband," and soon the Heidsieck dose was repeated. Wit, words, humor, laughter, and cross-firing began in fine style as the wine was doing its perfect work, and Prentice led the conversation with keen satire and thrusts all round the board. I could imagine myself seated at "the Club" with Dr. Sam Johnson, Garrick, Beauclerc, Goldsmith, and company, rattling away the hours in glorious jollity. The wine began to work upon my poetic memories, and I dashed into the arena like a gladiator from the gulches of Gaul, first spouting "The Closing Year" as a compliment to Prentice, and I must say that the poet and his friends seemed delighted at my rendition of his celebrated poem.

Prentice then began his badinage and spurred me about presuming to think that I was a poet, and finally defied me to write something offhand and prove to his friends that I was not a pretender.

I said, "All right; what shall I write about?" "Oh," said Prentice, "write about anything—write about us, wine, feasting fun, or philosophy." I asked for paper, and it was furnished. I then turned around to a side table, pulled my memories together, thought of Horace, the Falernian wine poet, and one of his odes, where he speaks of people joining you when you laugh, but declining to cling to you when you weep. Then, too, the suggestions of Prentice and the surrounding scene and anchored in my mind and inspired my lines.

I immediately pulled a pencil from my pocket and wrote the following verses inside of fifteen minutes, while my companions were dumping down wine with hilarious vociferation:

Laugh, and the world laughs with you,
Weep and you weep alone;
This grand old earth must borrow its mirth,
It has troubles enough of its own.
Sing, and the hills will answer;
Sigh, it is lost on the air;
The echoes bound to a joyful sound,
But shrink from voicing care.

Be glad, and your friends are many;
Be sad, and you lose them all;
There are none to decline your nectared wine,
But alone you must drink life's gall;
There is room in the halls of pleasure
For a long and a lordly train,
But one by one we must all file on
Through the narrow aisles of pain.

Feast, and your halls are crowded;
Fast, and the world goes by;
Succeed and give, 'twill help you live,
But no one can help you die.
Rejoice, and men will seek you;
Grieve, and they turn and go—
They want full measure of all your pleasure,
But they do not want your woe!

I threw these lines to Prentice. He read them to the revelers, and then exclaimed: "Si.," speaking to Miller, "didn't I tell you that fellow was a fool? Now I know he's crazy!"

Well, the world has had the benefit of my brain baby for thirty years, although "Exchange," "Anonymous," and other literary robbers have claimed it. What care I? Mankind can make the most of it. More than a dozen other of my verses have gone the rounds of the press under the colors of some plagiarist.

The glorious Prentice has slept beneath the sod for nearly a quarter of a century, but the grand thoughts that he uttered in life will spread over the years like perfume from an unseen censer and thrill the heart of mankind when the memory of his social and literary critics are washed into the waters of oblivion.

CHAPTER XI.

"PARSON" BROWNLOW.

WILLIAM G. BROWNLOW, of East Tennessee, was one of the most remarkable men I ever met. He was of slender build, six foot tall, high forehead, classic features, thin, firm lips, prominent, chiseled nose, and a bluish gray eye that was as direct and sure as death. He had what might be called a triangle head and countenance. He possessed the wisdom and truth of Socrates, the firmness and belief of Galilei, the bravery, and rashness of Winklereid, and the stolidity and fanaticism of John Brown,

He came from Virginia rural stock; rode the circuit as a mountain Methodist preacher, bestrode the tripod as an editor and wit, stood for the Union in the midst of the whirlpool of rebellion, graced the Governor's chair of his adopted State, and finally reached the United States Senate, where he shone like a landmark of loyalty and commanded the sincere respect of his greatest compeers.

No threat of chains or death could make him swerve from a position once taken, and at Knoxville, in the very teeth of armed rebel fury, after the fire on Fort Sumter, he belabored treason through the columns of the *Whig* with the most caustic castigation and abuse, and hoisted the Stars and Stripes over his home as a bold defiance to the Confederate troops that passed night and day by his door.

He courted the vengeance of Jeff. Davis, Secretary Benjamin, and General Crittenden, and even after the suppression of his paper, while in jail condemned to death by a drumhead court-martial, he wrote his scaffold speech and defied all the powers of the Confederacy. Such characters as John Brown, Abraham

Lincoln, and "Parson" Brownlow are met but once in a century, and only when universal wrong, like slavery, calls great moral heroes to the front.

I was introduced to Parson Brownlow by his son, Col. John Bell Brownlow, in the Marble Room of the Senate, when the old hero was suffering with physical ailments, being compelled, like another Radical—Thaddeus Stevens—to be wheeled about in an invalid's chair. His voice was clear and musical, his sentences clean cut as a razor, and his whole countenance pictured the ideal Puritan.

I spoke of being from Kentucky, whose mountain walls rose like barriers of loyalty on the boundary of his own beloved East Tennessee, where the Cumberland River winds its rushing way through those everlasting rock-ribbed heights of patriotism.

"Yes," he said, "I have always loved the people of Kentucky. I regarded Mr. Clay the greatest statesman America produced. Mr. Prentice, the poet and wit, too, I liked in my heart, although he and I crossed editorial lances sometimes with flashing acrimony. We warred in our papers, and while the *Journal* often struck me to the bone, I merely winced and tried to give back a Roland for an Oliver. Prentice had a loyal heart, while his family were rebels.

"I predicted and knew that secession and rebellion would fail, tried my best to convince its leaders, Davis, Yancy, Toombs, and Isham Harris, but they were hell-bent on breaking up the Union. I thought at times that the Abolitionists went too far; and I felt that while the Constitution and laws permitted slavery it should not be disturbed where it then existed, any more than any other property.

"But, when the flag on Sumter was shot down by defiant traitors and treason reared its horrible head, I could see nothing but the whole Union and its glorious history. From that moment to this I have staked my property, liberty, and life for the Nation, and had I ten thousand lives I would gladly give them all for the Union."

I remarked to him that East Tennessee never seceded.

"No!" said he, "so long as Smoky Mountain and Cumberland Mountain rear their pine-clad peaks to the sky and the waters of the Cumberland, French Broad, and Holston run down to the sea, so long will East Tennessee stand by the Union. We are patriots without price, and in proportion to our population sent more soldiers into the Union Army than any other spot in America. We are a simple and provincial people in our manners and habits, not garnishing our words or acts with hypocrisy. Our mountains and uplands are rugged, our valleys narrow but fertile, and a vein of genuine liberty, patriotism, and religion runs through the hearts of our people as true as the foresters of the Tyrol Swiss mountains."

"Senator," said I, "how did you feel when you went on the platform at Knoxville to answer William L. Yancy and his secession doctrine?"

"I felt, my dear sir, that some one ought to answer his false doctrine, and, as none of my neighbors wished to take the lead, I thought it my duty to do so. That was a wild mob audience, and I have wondered since that some of the young bloods did not shoot me.

"Yancy was very mad, and his black, flashing eyes shone upon me like those of a tiger, and while he seemed ready to leap at me he did not have the courage to do so. I was ready to die right there, and, as my Lord and Master wore the martyr's crown, I, too, was not unwilling to share his sacrifice for the everlasting principles of truth."

"May I ask if you really thought they would hang you the night you wrote your scaffold speech in the Knoxville jail?"

"Yes; I firmly believed that they would hang me at daylight. The drumhead court-martial tried me in my absence for treason! A good joke, wasn't it? Infernal traitors trying a patriot for treason; holding a court in hell, with Lucifer for judge. They were only too glad to send me to Nashville through the lines, and I believe it was a great relief to Davis, Benjamin, and Crittenden when they forced me, a lone, weary refugee, to leave their dastard dominions."

"But, Senator, did you not return to Nashville soon after the Harris legislature impulsively skedaddled?"

"Yes; that was a very funny scene. The first reports from Fort Donelson told in glowing colors how Buckner had captured Grant, and the whole town and rebel legislature got enthusiastically drunk, but the next day the boot was on the other leg, and Buell was reported to be advancing rapidly on the city of rocks. Great was the consternation and desire of the legislature to adjourn to a more congenial clime. Many places to the south were suggested. The Speaker at last brought down his gavel and said: 'If we never meet again in this world, I hope we shall meet in Heaven.'

"At this juncture a comical character from Hawkins County, named Bill Simpson, a Union man, who was loaded with liquid enthusiasm at the good news, staggered to the front and replied: 'Mr. Speaker, I hope this body will not adjourn to meet in Heaven, for they will never have a quorum there!'"

After a few more remarks I left the great patriot, shaking the hand of a man that had the faith of Peter the Hermit, Martin Luther, and Lorenzo Dow.

For many years he has slept in Gray Cemetery, overlooking the Holston River at Knoxville, and while the eagles of his mountain home soar into the upper blue and the waters of the French Broad dash down their rocky heights, his name will be revered, and the day is not distant when all the people of Tennessee will erect a splendid monument to the memory of a noble man who was true and faithful unto death.

Jim and John, the gallant sons of the grand old "Parson," raised regiments for the Union Army and commanded them on many a hard-fought field. John led the charge at Greenville, Tenn., on the morning of the 4th of September, 1864, that resulted in the death of the Confederate General John Morgan, of Kentucky.

In the month of July, 1864, Col. Jim Brownlow performed

one of the rarest and bravest acts of the civil war in crossing the Chattahooche River.

Maj. Gen. Ed. McCook, the illustrious cavalry officer of the Army of the Cumberland and late Governor of Colorado, makes the following statement in an official report July 9, 1864, to his superior officer :

A detachment, under Colonel Dorr, crossed the pontoon this afternoon and scouted the country in front of General Schofield. They found the enemy's cavalry there in force. Colonel Brownlow performed one of his characteristic feats today. I had ordered a detachment to cross at Cochran's Ferry. It was deep and he took them over naked; nothing but guns, cartridge boxes, and hats. They drove the enemy out of their rifle-pits, captured a non-commissioned officer and three men and the two boats on the other side. They would have got more, but the rebels had the advantage in running through the bushes and briars with their clothes on. It was certainly one of the funniest sights of the war, and a very successful raid for naked men to make.

Numerous anecdotes are told of the " Parson's " personal prowess. Hon. S. M. Arnell, late Congressman from Middle Tennessee and a friend of Brownlow, relates :

Some irate individual of Falstaffian courage, filled with the sour wine of State rights and secession, had busied himself in abusing Brownlow on the streets and elsewhere. At length he was served up in the *Whig* on live coals. This *bombastes furioso* proceeded to a store in the town to buy a cowhide. One was shown to him, but he objected to it, saying:

"It might be large enough for use on a mule or a horse, but I want a still larger one. I am going to use it on Brownlow."

The merchant said to him quietly:

"It is the largest one we have in the store; but I would advise you not to use it in the manner proposed."

"Why not?" he said snappishly. "Is he a fighting character?"

"No," responded the merchant; "among his neighbors he has the reputation of being a very quiet, peaceable man; but I know that he will not submit to a cowhiding."

"Well," said the snorting warrior, "he will have to stand it this time, for I am going to administer it."

So he started off in the direction of Brownlow's printing office.

There he was told that the editor had gone to the river to look after some lumber. He swaggered on in hot pursuit. Brownlow observed his coming. When the wordy duel began, Brownlow kept backing until he reached the water's edge, in which he had observed a long-handled mallet, such as lumbermen use. When the first stroke of the cowhide came down, he instantly seized the mallet and struck the assailant apparently lifeless at his feet. Feeling that he had repelled the insult, he did not strike a second blow. Some one passing by ran to the spot, picked up the apparently lifeless body, threw water into his face, and revived him sufficiently to place him in a sitting position against a log. At length, looking down on his bloody garments, then directly into the face of his opponent, who still remained, he blurted out:

"Well, you are a —— pretty preacher!"

"At any rate," responded Brownlow, "I am pretty successful. It has not taken me long to bring one mourner to the bench."

This prayer was kept standing in the *Whig* until it was suppressed by the Confederate authorities:

Almighty God, our Heavenly Father, in whose hands are the hearts of men and the issues of time and eternity, not mixed up with Locofocoism nor rendered offensive in Thy sight by being identified with men of corrupt minds, evil designs, and damnable purposes, such as are seeking to upturn the best Government on earth, Thou hast graciously promised to hear the prayers of those who in an humble spirit and with true faith—such as no secessionist can bring into exercise—call upon Thee. Be pleased, we beseech Thee, favorably to look upon and bless the Union men of this Commonwealth and sustain them in their praiseworthy efforts to perpetuate this Government and, under it, the institutions of our holy religion. Possess their minds with the spirit of true patriotism, enlightened wisdom and of persevering hostility toward those traitors, political gamblers, and selfish demagogues who are seeking to build up a miserable Southern Confederacy, and under it to inaugurate a new reading of the Ten Commandments, so as to teach that the chief end of man is nigger. In these days of trouble and perplexity, give the common people grace to perceive the right path, which, Thou knowest, leads from the camps of Southern madcaps and Northern copperheads, and enable them steadfastly to walk therein. So strengthen the common masses, O Lord, and so direct them that, they being hindered neither by the fear of fire-eaters nor by the love of the corrupt men in power, nor by bribery, nor by any overcharge of mean whisky, nor by any other Democratic passion, but being mindful of Thy constant superintendence, of the awful majesty of Thy righteousness, of Thy hatred of Democracy and its profligate leaders, and of the strict account they must hereafter give to Thee, they may, in counsel, word, and deed, aim supremely at the fulfillment of their duty, which is to talk, vote, and pray against the wicked leaders and ungodly advocates of secession. Grant that those of Thy professed ministers who are mixed up with with modern Democracy and have become so hardened in sin as to openly advocate the vile delusion may speedily abandon their unministerial ways or go over to the cause of the devil; that their positions may at least be unequivocal, and that they may thereby advance the welfare of the country! And grant that these fire-eaters may soon run their race; that the course of this world may be so peaceably ordered by Thy superintendence that Thy church and Thy whole people, irrespective of sects, may joyfully serve Thee, in all good conscience and godly quietness, through Jesus Christ, our Lord. Amen!

A gentleman in Arkansas wrote to the "Parson" and wished to know when he would join the Democratic party.

The following letter and reply will, no doubt, enlighten the reader, as it did Mr. Clark:

CAMDEN, ARK., *June* 30, 1860.

W. G. BROWNLOW.

DEAR SIR: I have learned with pleasure, upon what I consider reliable authority, that you have made up your mind to join the Democratic party and in the future act with us for the benefit of the country. When will you come out and announce it? It will have a good effect in the present election if you will make it known over your own signature.

Hoping to hear from you, I am very truly, yours,

JORDAN CLARK.

THE REPLY.

KNOXVILLE, TENN., *July* 6, 1860.

Mr. JORDAN CLARK.

DEAR SIR: I have your letter of June 30, and I hasten to let you know the precise time when I expect to come out and formally announce that I have joined the Democratic party. When the sun shines at midnight and the moon at midday; when man forgets to be selfish or Democrats lose their inclination to steal; when nature stops her onward march to rest, or all the water courses in America flow up stream; when flowers lose their odor and trees shed no leaves; when birds talk and beasts of burden laugh; when damned spirits swap hell for Heaven with the angels of light and pay them the boot in mean whisky; when impossibilities are in fashion and no proposition is too absurd to be believed—then you may credit the report that I have joined the Democratic party.

I join the Democrats! Never; so long as there are sects in churches, weeds in gardens, fleas in hog pens, dirt in victuals, disputes in families, wars with nations, water in the ocean, bad men in America, or base women in France. No, Jordan Clark, you may hope, you may congratulate, you may reason, you may sneer, but that cannot be. The thrones of the Old World, the courts of the universe, the governments of men, may all fall and crumble into ruin; the New World may commit the national suicide of dissolving this Union, but all this and more must occur before I join the Democracy.

I join the Democrats! Jordan Clark, you know not what you say. When I join Democracy, the Pope of Rome will join the Methodist Church. When Jordan Clark, of Arkansas, is president of the Republic of Great Britain, by the universal suffrage of a contented people; when Queen Victoria consents to be divorced from Prince Albert by a county court in Kansas; when Congress obliges by law James Buchanan to marry an European princess; when the Pope leases the Capitol at Washington for his city residence; when Alexander of Russia and Napoleon of France are elected Senators in Congress from New Mexico; when good men cease to go to Heaven or bad men to hell; when this world is turned upside down; when proof is afforded, clear and unquestionable, that there is no God; when men turn to ants, and ants to elephants—then I will change my political faith and come out on the side of Democracy!

Supposing that this full and frank letter will enable you to fix upon the period when I will come out a full-grown Democrat, and requesting you to communicate the same to all whom it may concern in Arkansas, I am, yours truly,

W. G. BROWNLOW.

The following address, written to his countrymen under the shadow of the scaffold while in the Knoxville jail, is unparalleled, save by the speech of Robert Emmet before his sentence of death by the minion of a tyrant:

FELLOW-COUNTRYMEN: I have often addressed many of you upon different topics, but never under circumstances like those which now surround me, as I feel that I am speaking for the last time. I suppose I have been sentenced to hang by a court-martial sitting in this city; I say I suppose so, for I have never had any trial, or even a notice of a trial being in progress. It is alike a matter of indifference whether I was tried by that court-martial in my absence and in the absence of witnesses and counsel, or whether I had been present; the result would have been death. Justice at the hands of such unmitigated scoundrels and ruffians is the last thing I would expect. Indeed, there is more glory in being put to death by such men than in being acquitted, after going through the forms of trial.

Fellow-countrymen, I am shortly to be executed—not for any crime, but for my devotion to my country, her laws and Constitution. I die for refusing to espouse the cause of this wicked rebellion; and I glory in it, strange as you may think it. I could have lived, if I had taken an oath of allegiance to this so-called Confederacy. Rather than stultify myself and disgrace my family by such an oath, I agree to die. I never could sanction this so-called government, and I trust that no child of mine will ever do it. * * * I have a word to say as to my family. I want the minds of my wife and children impressed with what is true—that they are not disgraced, but honored by my death. Let me be shrouded in the sacred folds of the star-spangled banner; and let my children's children know that the last words I uttered on earth were—

" Forever float that standard sheet!
Where breathes the foe, but falls before us,
With Freedom's soil beneath our feet,
And Freedom's banner streaming o'er us!"

CHAPTER XII.

FATHER RYAN AND HENRY STANTON.
TWO SOUTHERN POETS.

REV. ABRAM J. RYAN, the poet priest of the South, was a remarkable genius in the way of alliterative lines and poetic periods. He was born in Norfolk, Va., studied for the priesthood, and lived for many years in Mobile, Ala. When the civil war broke out he threw his fortunes with the Confederacy and remained as a chaplain to the close of the conflict, ministering alike to friend and foe on the bloody battlefields of the rebellion.

In the winter of 1868 I met the illustrious prelate and poet at Barnum's Hotel, in Baltimore, after one of his lectures in the Monumental City.

He possessed a fine form, round, broad head, long, dark hair, and large bluish gray eyes, and a countenance as open and devoted as the dawn. Benevolence shone in every lineament of his full face, yet at intervals a melancholy shade o'erhung his brow.

In company with a few of his friends we adjourned to a private parlor and had a social seance that lasted until the clock in the tower struck the midnight hour. His two friends had served with him during the war, and of course many fond recollections were called to mind; and, while I served and bled on the battlefield for "Uncle Sam," it put no damper on the talk of these Southern warriors.

The ease with which Father Ryan received and entertained me may be accounted for by the fact that he and my uncle, Father John Joyce, of Maysville, Ky., were very intimate friends for many years.

We requested the genial and generous priest to recite to us some of his noted productions, and without hesitation he delivered—

THE CONQUERED BANNER.

" Furl that banner, for 'tis weary,
Round its staff 'tis drooping dreary—
Furl it, fold it, it is best;
For there's not a man to wave it,
And there's not a sword to save it,
And there's not one left to love it
In the blood which heroes gave it;
And its foes now scorn and brave it;
Furl it, hide it, let it rest.

" Take the banner down! 'tis tattered;
Broken is its staff and shattered;
And the valiant hosts are scattered
Over whom it floated high.
Oh! 'tis hard for us to fold it,
Hard to think there's none to hold it;
Hard that those who once unrolled it
Now must furl it with a sigh.

" Furl that banner, furl it sadly!
Once ten thousand hailed it gladly
And ten thousand wildly, madly,
Swore it should forever wave,
Swore that foeman's sword should never
Hearts like theirs entwined dissever
Till that flag should float forever
O'er their freedom or their grave.

" Furl it, for the hands that grasped it
And the hearts that fondly clasped it,
Cold and dead are lying low;
And that banner—it is trailing,
While around it sounds the wailing
Of its people and their woe.

" For, though conquered, they adore it!
Love the cold, dead hands that bore it!
Weep for those who fell before it!

>   Pardon those who trailed and tore it!
>   But, oh! wildly they deplore it,
>   We who furl and fold it so.
>
> "Furl that banner; true 'tis gory;
>   Yet it's wreathed around with glory,
>   And 'twill live in song and story,
>   Though its folds are in the dust;
>   For its fame on brightest pages
>   Penned by poets and by sages,
>   Shall go sounding down the ages—
>   Furl its folds though now we must!
>
> "Furl that banner, softly, slowly!
>   Treat it gently—it is holy—
>   For it droops above their head—
>   Touch it not—unfurl it never,
>   Let it droop there, furled forever—
>   For its people's hopes are dead!"

HENRY T. STANTON is the son of Hon. Richard Stanton, of Maysville, Ky., who was a distinguished lawyer and a member of Congress before the late civil war.

When a boy, attending school at my uncle's cathedral, I remember the embryo poet in connection with some of my playmates, who were of the Pierce, Pointz, Goddard, and Armstong families.

More than thirty years from school days had elapsed in 1886, when I made a lecture tour through Kentucky, taking in Owingsville, Mount Sterling, Winchester, Carlisle, Paris, Lexington, Frankfort, and Louisville. While staying at the Capital Hotel, at Frankfort, I learned through Gen. Dexter Keogh that the poet Stanton was connected with the superintendent of public instructions and had an office in the Capitol building. We called on the jolly, round, and genial genius and spent a pleasant hour discoursing about old times at Maysville, and naturally drifted into literary topics. I referred to the poet's books and praised in no unmeasured terms his celebrated poem, "The Moneyless Man," and requested him to recite it. He repeated it as follows in a very impressive manner; and I must say, right here, that I fail to find in all human literature a more incisive, truthful, pathetic, and philosophic poem :

"Is there no place on the face of the earth
Where charity dwelleth, where virtue has birth,
Where bosoms in mercy and kindness will heave,
Where the poor and the wretched shall ask and receive?
Is there no place at all where a knock from the poor
Will bring a kind angel to open the door?
Ah! search the wide world wherever you can,
There's no open door for a moneyless man.

"Go look in yon hall, where the chandelier's light
Drives off with its splendor the darkness of night,
Where the rich hanging velvet in shadowy fold
Sweeps gracefully down with its trimmings of gold.
And the mirrors of silver take up and renew
In long lighted vistas the wildering view!
Go there at the banquet and find if you can
A welcoming smile for a moneyless man.

"Go look in yon church of the cloud-reaching spire,
Which gives to the sun his same look of red fire,
Where the arches and columns are gorgeous within,
And the walls seem as pure as a soul without sin;
Walk down the long isle; see the rich and the great
In the pomp and the pride of their worldly estate;
Walk down in your patches and find, if you can,
Who opens a pew to a moneyless man.

"Go look in the banks, where Mammon has told
His hundreds and thousands in silver and gold;
Where safe from the hands of the starving and poor
Lies pile upon pile of the glittering ore.
Walk up to the counter; ah! there you may stay
Till your limbs grow old, till your hairs grow gray;
And you'll find at the banks not one of the clan
With money to loan to a moneyless man.

"Go look at yon judge in his dark flowing gown,
With the scales wherein law weigheth equity down;
Where he frowns on the weak and smiles on the strong,

And punishes right while he justifies wrong;
Where juries their lips to the Bible have laid
To render a verdict they've already made—
Go there in the court-room and find, if you can,
Any law for the cause of a moneyless man.

" Then go to your hovel—no raven has fed
The wife who has suffered too long for her bread;
Kneel down by her pallet and kiss the death frost
From the lips of the angel your poverty lost;
Then turn in your agony upward to God,
And bless, while it smites you, the chastening rod,
And you'll find at the end of your life's little span—
There's a welcome above for the moneyless man!"

CHAPTER XIII.

JOHN C. BRECKINRIDGE.

JOHN CABELL BRECKINRIDGE was born near Lexington, Ky., on the 21st of January, 1821. His ancestors were from Virginia, and his grandfather was Attorney-General under the administration of President Jefferson, and afterwards a United States Senator from the State of Kentucky. Breckinridge received a classical education at Center College, Danville, and studied law at Transylvania University, Lexington.

He practiced his profession successfully for years before the Mexican war, and participated in that conflict toward its close as major of the Third Kentucky Infantry Volunteers. On his return from the Army he was elected to the State legislature and afterward nominated for Congress, defeating by a narrow majority the celebrated Leslie Combs, boy captain of the war of 1812. He next defeated Governor Letcher, riding triumphantly over every political competitor, the young Democracy of his district rallying their forces against the best blood of the old Whigs, who had been so successful under the leadership of Henry Clay.

Breckinridge was about six feet one, muscular form, straight as an arrow, high round forehead, bluish gray eyes, firm lips and chin, and a sonorous musical voice that sent its ringing tones to the outer edge of an audience. The rising and falling inflections of his voice, where anger or pathos was intended, combined with magnetic gesticulation, acted on the listeners like some spiritual spell, swaying the mind and even body with the wand of a master of universal eloquence.

A few years after the Mexican war the State of Kentucky

voted an appropriation of several thousand dollars to exhume and bring back the bodies of her heroic sons who fell on the plains and mountains of Mexico. A magnificent marble shaft, fifty feet high, resting on a broad pedestal, with the names of the soldiers and officers inscribed thereon, was in due time unveiled at the romantic cemetery in Frankfort, the capital of the State.

John C. Breckinridge was selected to deliver the eulogium over the remains of his dead comrades. With words of burning eloquence and mournful memories he inspired the patriotism of the assembled multitude, and those who heard his grand oration will never forget its lofty periods and sententious philosophy.

Theodore O'Harra was selected to deliver the poem, "The Bivouac of the Dead," one of the finest tributes in English literature to the memory of dead soldiers—a classic thought that will shine down the ages and thrill the hearts of mankind with patriotic veneration for those who fight and fall for home and country. These lines will be immortal:

> " Rest on, embalmed and sainted dead,
>   Dear as the blood ye gave!
> No impious footsteps here shall tread
>   The herbage of your grave;
> Nor shall your glory be forgot
>   While fame her record keeps,
> Or Honor points the hallowed spot
>   Where Valor proudly sleeps.
>
> Yon marble minstrel's voiceless stone,
>   In deathless song shall tell,
> When many a vanished year hath flown,
>   The story how ye fell;
> Nor wreck nor change nor winter's blight,
>   Nor Time's remorseless doom,
> Can dim one ray of holy light
>   That gilds your glorious tomb!"

On the 4th of July, 1886, I visited the Frankfort Cemetery in company with General Dexter Keogh and pondered at celebrated tombs around the great monument, such as Daniel Boone, Colonels McKee and Clay, and the Celtic poet, O'Harra. I penciled these lines to the latter's memory:

> I stood at the grave of O'Harra,
>   And plucked a sweet clover in bloom;
> Sent a sigh to the soul of the poet,
>   And wept over Memory's tomb.
>
> I heard in the voice of the forest
>   The songs that the poets would sing,
> And caught every tone of his lyre,
>   Like the whirr of a bird on the wing.
>
> Yet sadly I sighed for O'Harra,
>   And knelt at the shrine of his fame,
> And longed for the holy communion
>   That circled the sound of his name!

In the halls of Congress Breckinridge took the stand of a leader at once, although barely of legal age. His affability, generosity, and manly sentiments endeared him even to his opponents, and while his Democracy was unquestioned he never hit the enemy below the belt or shot the poisoned arrows of spite. What he said and did was above board, and while the petty politicians of his party might strike with the dagger of an assassin he wielded the claymore of conscience and conviction.

Breckinridge was a generous and lavish entertainer of friends and the public. He was a particular favorite of the ladies. His manly form, bright eye, and eloquent tongue fascinated all who met him, and had his lot been cast about the waters of the Golden Horn he might have been a Grand Vizier and led a corps of Oriental beauties in his royal train!

On the death of Henry Clay at the National Hotel, Washington, fn June, 1852, Breckinridge announced the sad event to his compeers in Congress. Although many eulogies were delivered in the Senate and House by noted Whigs and Democrats, there were none that struck a loftier flight than that of the youg Mirabeau from the Lexington district in memory of the sage of Ashland. This tribute to the memory of the great Clay might be truthfully uttered over the remains of Breckinridge himself:

In him intellect, person, eloquence, and courage united to form a character fitted to command. He fired with his own enthusiasm and controlled by his amazing will individuals and masses. No reverse could crush his spirit, nor defeat reduce him to despair.

And to cap the climax of the eulogium the orator, like an an eagle, soars thusly into the Alpine crags of thought:

The glory of his great actions shed a mellow luster on his declining years, and, to fill the measure of his fame, his countrymen, weaving for him the laurel wreath, with common hands bind it about his venerable brows and send him crowned to history.

Breckinridge, like a well-rooted white ash of his native State, continued to grow in political power, and was nominated and elected Vice President of the United States in conjunction with President Buchanan. As presiding officer of the Senate he gave the greatest satisfaction to both parties and held the scales of justice with an unbiased hand.

The Presidential campaign of 1860 found him the champion of his party, carrying the laurels away from the "Little Giant" Douglass in the Charleston Convention, where Democracy broke in twain and made the election of Abraham Lincoln certain— another case of a house divided against itself, and the usual result of failure.

The winter and spring of 1860 and 1861 found the Congress of the United States and the whole country in the seething throes of impulsive rebellion. State after State in the South passed ordinances of secession, withdrawing their allegiance from the Union, and finally elected Jefferson Davis and Mr. Alex. Stephens executive officers of the new Confederacy. Sections and platoons of Southern Senators and Representatives withdrew from their seats in Congress, after a futile attempt to convince the North of the justice of their cause. Officers of the regular Army and Navy, imitating the examples of Generals

Lee and Twiggs and Commodore Buchanan and Captain Semmes, severed their connection with the Government and rushed into the wild vortex of rebellion. Senator John J. Crittenden, from Kentucky, and a large number of his compeers offered a compromise, but to no purpose, and soon the abortive neutrality of Kentucky was swept aside, when citizens enlisted directly for the Union or Confederacy. Breckinridge remained about Washington as long as he could, but soon Powell and himself saw that action was imperatively necessary, and they returned to Kentucky in the spring of 1861.

Lincoln was now at the national helm, and poor old Buchanan had gone to grass in the Keystone State, like another broken Wolsey, who "fell like Lucifer, never to hope again" from the public, his master.

The summer and fall of 1861 found Kentucky a camping ground of war, with its citizens divided against each other to the death, brother against brother and father against son—the terrible situation of civil war. Gens. Humphrey Marshall and "Cerro Cordo" Williams had established a Confederate camp at Prestonsburgh, in the mountains near the Virginia line, and Gen. William Nelson had established a Union camp on the Kentucky River, near Nicholasville, and "Camp Dick Robinson," near Danville, where the cavalry and infantry for the Government could organize for fight. Gen. Simon Boliver Buckner also established camps for Confederates at Bowling Green and Russellville. A Union camp was established at the Olympian Springs, in Bath County, where the Twenty-fourth Kentucky was organized under the command of Col. L. B. Grigsby and Major J. S. Hurt, who afterward commanded the regiment to the close of the rebellion.

Matters were getting very hot as the summer of 1861 proceeded, and Breckinridge knew it was time to leave his State and enlist for the Confederacy, most of his political confreres having already gone over the mountains to join their friends in Virginia. Like Lee, his heart was never in favor of breaking up the Union, but past personal and political associations drew him like a magnet into all the future hardships and failures of the civil war and kept him there to the end as General and Secretary of War, but, like Bolingbroke, he was finally compelled to wander for many years as an exile in foreign lands.

His escape with four companions after the fall of the Confederacy, in April, 1865, through the forests of Carolina and Georgia, the rivers and everglades of Florida, and 200 miles in an open boat across the stormy Gulf of Mexico to Cuba, reads more like a Viking romance than a reality.

The last speech made by Breckinridge on his way to Virginia to join the Confederacy was delivered at Mount Sterling, Ky. People from the surrounding counties came to hear what the champion of the Southern cause might say. He spoke in the court-house for more than two hours to a large and sympathetic audience. About the close of his remarks I elbowed my way through the crowd to hear the orator, not that I sympathized with the meeting, but to listen to a famous man. His peroration was a flash of impassioned eloquence and made the deepest impression on the great mass meeting. It was indelibly impressed on my mind, and was uttered in about these words :

And now, Kentuckians, I appeal to you to stand by your State and your Southern brothers, who have taken up the gauge of battle to hurl back the Goths and Vandals of the North, who are now marching down to desolate our sacred soil and murder our people in the name of liberty. Do not be deceived that this war will be a holiday affair, or that the enemy will falter until their last man and dollar are thrown into the vortex of this civil conflict. Be not deluded that one Southern gentleman can whip five Yankees. I tell you now that each one of Lincoln's soldiers will be a match for any of our men, and that man is a fool who underrates the power of the North and its unlimited resources. Yet, with right on our side, in defense of our property and people, and the god of battles smiling on the cause of the just, I have an abiding faith that we shall achieve our independence and cut loose from the Abolition conclave of the North, who are determined to free our slaves and make them the equal of their masters. Nature and her laws never made the black man the equal of the white, and all the power of our enemies, now or hereafter, shall never make us consent to the outrageous and unnatural proposition.

Kentucky has never flinched on the field of battle. From the early pioneer days of the red savage at Fort Bryan and Blue Lick to the snowy fields of the River Raisin in Canada, the cotton bags at New Orleans, the waters of Tippecanoe, the everglades of Florida, the plains of Buena Vista on to the halls of the Montezumas, the bones of our fearless and valiant people lie bleaching as a grand testimonial to their bravery and patriotism. I implore you, then, my beloved Kentuckians, to rouse up your slumbering energies, shake up your lion hearts, and come to the rescue of your native land.

In the summer of 1872 I spent ten days at the West End Hotel, at Long Branch, with my family. General Breckinridge happened to be staying at the same hotel, enjoying the bathing, driving, racing, and social cheer that clustered around that noted watering place. He had but recently returned from exile, and after a separation of eleven years we renewed the introduction of Col. Thomas Johnson, of Mount Sterling. We naturally gravitated together, for it is a well-known fact that, while Kentuckians are eminently hospitable and friendly to strangers, there is a clannishness and State pride among themselves that no enmity can blighten and no sorrow or defeat chill or destroy. The land of fair women, fast horses, brave men, and pure whisky challenges mankind for its match, and so long as its limestone formation remains and its everlasting springs run to the sea the Blue Grass State will be found at the front with its generous heart and hand held out to all the world.

The General, myself, and family became very intimate, and with bathing, driving, dining, and attending the summer races at Monmouth Park, our time was spent in a round of profitable pleasure. He was courted on all sides, and whenever he appeared on the porches, balconies, clubs, or race tracks the world seemed to recognize an illustrious man. Evening after evening we'd chat after dinner, or walk over to "Daily's" or "Chamberlain's" clubs to while away a few hours in meeting old friends or taking a turn at the wheel of fortune to pay for the fine bird suppers of these noted entertainers.

One morning the General asked me to walk over to Grant's cottage, only a few blocks away, saying that he had never met the President. At the time I occupied a public office under General Grant and was on friendly terms with him. On our route I called at the cottage of Gen. O. E. Babcock and asked him to accompany us to see the President. It was about 11 o'clock in the morning when we were ushered in through the center hall and out on the broad porch, where I found General Grant alone, smoking and reading a newspaper. I introduced him to General Breckinridge, when we were asked to be seated, and for an hour or more these two noted men talked of the past and current events as if nothing had disturbed the equanimity of their historic recollections. Before taking our departure "Jerry" brought in three mint julips, and Breckinridge proposed a toast to the United States, which we drank standing.

The night before I left Long Branch for the West Breckinridge and myself had been over at Chamberlain's until after midnight. On our return to the hotel he asked me to sit down on the porch and look upon the roaring ocean and the brilliant stars that glittered in their eternal realm. His heart was seemingly surcharged with the memories of vanished years, for he spoke pathetically and eloquently for more than an hour. I, too, referred to the past and particularly to his speech at Mount Sterling, concluding by asking him how he really felt as to the result of the war. "Ah," said he, "Joyce, it is all right and far better that we still live as one people than be torn into fragments by the minions of princes, kings, and emperors. Many a lonely hour I have spent in midnight moments on the streets of London and Paris awaiting the time that I could once again catch a glimpse of the Stars and Stripes, the flag of my fathers, and all I now wish is to sleep forever beneath its God-given folds."

His wish has been granted. For many years the suns of

summer and the snows of winter have enwrapped his sacred dust at Lexington, Ky., under the shadow of the magnificent monument erected to the memory of his friend, Henry Clay; and his own heroic statue stands in front of the court house that once echoed to his eloquent periods in behalf of liberty and justice.

> " Green be the turf above thee,
> Friend of my better days;
> None knew thee but to love thee,
> Nor named thee but to praise!"

CHAPTER XIV.

GEN. NATHANIEL BEDFORD FORREST.

THE eagle of the air, the tiger of the land, and the shark of the sea are by nature made for combat and are instruments of destruction in the hands of that Mysterious Power that rules the globe and all the unknown worlds beyond the sun and stars.

So are some men created natural warriors for the destruction of their fellows, like Alexander the Great, Napoleon Bonaparte, "Stonewall" Jackson, Phil. Sheridan, and Forrest, the slave trader. Yet Alexander was trained for war under the eye of his illustrious father, Philip of Macedon. Napoleon was schooled in the Military Institute of France, while Forrest, one of the greatest cavalry officers of the late Confederacy, was reared on a farm with an axe, a plough, and a horse as training instruments of his military glory and received only the bare rudiments of a country education.

Forrest was a magnetic man, standing stalwart and erect, six feet one inch, broad shouldered, long arms, high round forehead, dark gray eyes, a prominent nose, emphatic jaw, compressed lips and a mustache, setting off a face that said to all the world, " Out of my way, I'm coming ! "

His step was firm, action impulsive, voice sonorous, and, taken all in all, there was not a soldier of the Confederacy that acted with more celerity or effective force from the 14th of June, 1861, when he became a private at Memphis, to the 9th of June, 1865, at Gainesville, Ala., where he surrendered as Lieutenant General to the United States authorities.

To determine with Forrest was to act, and the flash of his saber at the head of his column, charging the cavalry or infantry of the enemy, inspired his troops with the sunlight of victory, and they dashed into battle like the audacious warriors of Napoleon on the field of Austerlitz.

Forrest was born at Chapel Hill, Bedford County, Tenn., on the 13th of July, 1821. His paternal ancestors came from England and Scotland, while his maternal were of Irish blood.

When sixteen years of age his father died, leaving a widow and ten children, our subject being the eldest, who at once took charge of a farm in Mississippi and assisted his plucky mother to rear the weak brood that looked to them for support. Work was so imperative that young Forrest had but little chance for an education, attending for a few winter months the log schoolhouses of his rural section, where the teachers knew little more than their pupils.

Country sports, such as dances, barbecues, horse races, and sometimes feud fights were all the recreations that Nathan indulged in, yet whenever he appeared in a fight or a horse race he invariably came out victorious.

At the age of twenty-five Forrest married Mary Ann Montgomery, a direct descendant of the gallant Irish general who fell on the heights of Quebec in December, 1775.

While living at Hernando, Miss., in March, 1845, doing a general trading business, he was attacked on the public square by four planters for some quarrel that he had assumed for an uncle. Thirteen shots were exchanged. Forrest wounded three of his assailants and drove the other from the field. He moved to Memphis in 1852, and began trading in real estate and continued cotton planting and slave trading. About this time he was blown up in a steamboat, but providentially escaped, while sixty other pasengers were lost.

The most heroic thing ever done by Forrest was his rescue of young Abel, who had killed a friend in a family quarrel, from the hands of a Memphis mob of 3,000 infuriated men, who dragged the boy from jail, swung a rope around his neck, and were on the point of hoisting him over a beam when this intrepid citizen rushed through the frantic crowd, drew his Bowie knife, cut the rope, and hurried the intended victim back to jail, where the mob followed and still demanded blood.

Forrest jumped upon the jail steps, drew a revolver, and swore he would kill the first man that attempted to enter, and then and there that lone hero with truth and law on his side conquered a howling, desperate mob! There was nothing in his subsequent career that equaled this for desperate, sublime courage—such as Winkleried displayed when he threw himself on the Austrian spears or Leonidas blocking the pass of Thermopylæ with his his immortal three hundred.

I was introduced to General Forrest and Col. Roger Hanson at Mount Sterling, Ky., in the summer of 1861, where he came to secretly recruit for the Southern Army and procure arms. He was a splendid specimen of manhood, and no wonder some of the chivalric Kentucky bloods followed him back to Tennessee, where he led them and thousands of others in many a hard-fought battle.

Forrest was in the trap of Fort Donelson the night before Buckner surrendered to the unconquerable Grant, but before daylight he escaped with his command through the Federal lines like a hawk evading the swoop of an eagle.

For more than two years after this event he participated in all the great battles of the West and South, charging with recklessness at Shiloh, dashing and ubiquitous at Chickamauga, desperate and successful at Murfreesboro and Franklin, until his final surrender as Lieutenant General of the vanquished Confederacy. His successful dash into Memphis in the face of Federal power, his capture of gunboats with a cavalry force, and his destruction of military stores are familiar to the historian. The only blot upon his escutcheon as a soldier is the massacre of the blacks at Fort Pillow, which has been laid directly at the door of General Chalmers, Forrest's subordinate, although denied by that officer.

One great secret of General Forrest's success can be traced to the keen knowledge he had of men, for in the selection of his subordinates, such as Wheeler, Pegram, Chalmers, Bell, Buford, Rucker, Lyon, Jackson, Roddy, Wirt, Adams, and the dashing Gen. Frank Armstrong, he displayed great military genius, securing men who had their heart in their work and were willing at a moment's notice, in sunshine or storm, to die for their cause and commander. The immediate staff of General Forrest were also as loyal as death and never hesitated to carry an order to the most perilous point of battle. Such is the stuff that real soldiers are made of, whether fighting in the Macedonian phalanx with Alexander, in the legions of Cæsar, the squares of Napoleon, the columns of Skobeleff, or the corps of Grant and Lee. Long live the real heroic soldier, who fights and dies for what he believes the right in any land or clime! They have ever been monumented in marble and bronze in all ages, and shall be while mankind honors truth and valor.

I met Forrest a short time before he died, at the Overton House, in Memphis, and talked over the late war, reminding him of our first meeting at Mount Sterling. He spoke with a measured, melancholy tone, and asked me during the conversation what I thought his most successful military achievement.

I told him frankly that his military order disbanding his soldiers, the last to surrender, at Gainesville on the 9th of May, a month after Lee's surrender, was the best act of his life! He smiled, a far-off smile, and said "All right."

The following sentences from his farewell order will show the truth and courage of the man: "Soldiers, that we are beaten is a self-evident fact, and any further resistance on our part would be justly regarded as the very height of folly and rashness. * * * The terms of our surrender manifest a spirit of magnanimity and liberality on the part of the Federal authorities, which should be met on our part by a faithful compliance with all the stipulations and conditions therein expressed! * * * You have been good soldiers; you can be good citizens. Obey the laws, preserve your honor, and the Government to which you have surrendered can afford to be, and will be magnanimous!"

These are noble words, from an honest and heroic foe, and they should be memorized and pasted in the sombrero of some of the soldiers and citizens who followed in the wake of the "lost cause."

I fought for more than three years against General Forrest and his courageous comrades, and under like circumstance would gladly do so again, but I can say truthfully that I never met a genuine, blood-battlefield Confederate soldier that was sorry for the death of slavery or the re-establishment of our God-given Union!

> Over the ashes of Forrest
> Let flowers of freshness wave;
> He was faithful, bold, and honest—
> Generous, manly, and brave!

CHAPTER XV.

"CORPORAL" TANNER.

I FIRST met James Tanner ten years ago at a banquet given by the Knights of St. Patrick at the Academy of Music in Brooklyn, N. Y.

Thomas Kinsella, the editor of the *Eagle*, was the president of the association and one of the most popular men in the City of Churches. Some 300 guests sat down at the feast. Among the set speakers for the evening were Mayor Lowe, Henry Ward Beecher, Stewart L. Woodford, "Corporal" Tanner, myself, and others.

Mayor Lowe's speech to the "City of Brooklyn" was pointed, concise, and intelligent. Beecher's speech on "Religion" was faultless, philosophic, and grand. General Woodford, to the "President of the United States," spoke with intense eloquence. "Corporal" Tanner launched away in sonorous style in eulogistic terms of the "Union Soldiers" and received spontaneous applause, while I wound up the formal toasts in a compliment to "Woman."

I was much impressed with the "Corporal," having heard of him so often in connection with Grand Army encampments and as the constant and never-failing friend of a soldier.

At the age of seventeen, in 1861, he enlisted from his father's farm, in Schoharie County, in the Eighty-seventh New York Regiment. He served under the heroic Phil. Kearney, and at the second battle of Bull Run had both of his feet blown off, and from that day to this, more than thirty-two years, has suffered untold torture, uncomplaining as an ancient philosopher.

For many years he was collector of taxes for the city of Brooklyn, and gave universal satisfaction to his fellow-citizens.

He has also lectured on several occasions for Grand Army and social circles, and has never failed to interest his audience or elicit their generous applause.

"Corporal" Tanner stands about five feet ten, stalwart in body, with a large round head, set firmly on square shoulders, and crowned with a suit of stubborn gray hair. His eyes are of a bluish gray, prominent nose, firm lips surmounted with a bristling mustache, emphatic chin, and a full, open countenance that would attract any beholder.

In the Harrison campaign in Indiana he did more to carry the State for his party chief than any man in that Commonwealth, for wherever he was advertised to speak the old soldiers turned out *en masse* to hear the noted corporal.

For this service the leaders of the Republican party insisted that President Harrison should appoint him Pension Commissioner, which was finally done. His love for the old soldiers, whose claims had lain for so long in the pigeon-holes of the Department, from two to twenty-five years, soon showed itself in a speedy settlement of thousands of meritorious cases. But his liberal and generous construction of the pension laws in re-rating and increasing their allowance soon brought down upon his devoted head the criticism of former foes, political cowards and bloated bondholders, men who took advantage of the Government's necessity in its financial strait while "Corporal" Tanner and his comrades rushed to the battlefield and lost their health, blood, and life for the preservation of this God-given Union.

President Harrison listened to the howl and growl of the rabble, while the Secretary of the Interior and his assistant lent aid to the cry, and finally forced the "Corporal" to resign.

Since then he has been engaged as pension attorney in prosecuting the claims of old soldiers, and has been very successful in his avocation.

I have never met a more generous or benevolent man than "Corporal" Tanner, and if his power and pocket were as big as his brave heart every soldier who fought for the Stars and Stripes would receive at least a dollar a day to help him over the corduroy roads of old age and pathetic poverty.

The "Corporal" is direct in all his movements. He is a man with a forgiving spirit and without malice. For those who once wore the "gray" he now shows the kindest regard. Not long ago, Gen. John B. Gordon, a gallant Confederate soldier from Georgia, delivered his celebrated lecture on "The Last Days of the Confederacy" for the benefit of the disabled soldiers of the Union Veteran Legion and the Confederate home in Richmond. "Corporal" Tanner, as the commander of the Legion, introduced the gallant Confederate to 10,000 people assembled in Convention Hall, at Washington, and Gen. John M. Schofield, the Commander of the United States Army, presided with his usual dignity and intelligence.

This auspicious event, a union meeting of the "blue" and the "gray" was mainly brought about by "Corporal" Tanner, whose magnanimity to a fallen foe is as conspicuous as his bravery was against a standing one. When he passes away, beyond the mountain ranges of this life, the soldiers of the Republic will lose one of their best friends, and his family and neighbors a generous father and faithful man. Tanner never had time enough to tell a lie or garnish his acts with the parsley of hypocrisy, and his whole nature pivots on "friendship," "charity," and "loyalty"—the bed-rock doctrine of the Grand Army of the Republic.

CHAPTER XVI.

THE NATIONAL CAPITAL.

THE milestones of memory clustering around the National Capital are rich with historic lore and refreshing to the tourist from every land and clime.

Stand with me for a moment at the Scott statue, on the heights of the National Soldiers' Home, to the north of Washington, as the slanting beams of evening irradiate the scene. Far to the right and west the rolling hills of the Old Dominion lift their pine-clad crests over the troubled waters of the upper Potomac, and on a nearer view the towers and turrets of the Jesuit University shine over Georgetown Heights like Alpine sentinels guarding the vales below. The forest trees of Oak Hill and Arlington nod their emerald heads to the view, while the winds of nature sing a mournful requiem over the citizen soldiers who have gone into camp on the upland slopes of Omnipotence.

Oak Hill contains the dust of many illustrious men. Chase, Governor and Secretary of the Treasury, slept there until removed to Cincinnati; Stanton, the great War Secretary and iron arm of the rebellion, rests under a tall granite shaft that is not more firm or compact than the heroic character it memorializes. Gen. Reno, who fell at South Mountain, finds peace beneath a broken marble column. Captain Morris, of Monitor, Merrimac, and Cumberland memory, mingles here with Mother Earth, and as long as the waters of Hampton Roads shall tumble their white caps to the sea his heroic and patriotic conduct will be cherished by a grateful country.

Lorenzo Dow, the great apostle of temperance and revival religion, is covered with a sandstone slab, grown over with lichens and creeping grasses. Bishop Pinckney, the celebrated Episcopalian, has a life-size marble statue over his grave, erected by the benevolence of W. W. Corcoran, the millionaire, who sleeps beneath a marble pagoda across the hill from his sacerdotal friend. John Howard Payne, author of "Home, Sweet Home," has a monument and marble bust to glorify his dust in death, while in life he was a poor, forlorn wanderer, often without home, food, or shelter.

> When I am dead let no vain pomp display
> A surface sorrow o'er my pulseless clay,
> But all the dear old friends I loved in life
> May shed a tear, console my child and wife.
>
> When I am dead some sage for self-renown
> May urn my ashes in some park or town,
> And give when I am cold and lost and dead
> A marble shaft where once I needed bread!

I could not help quoting these few lines from my book, "Peculiar Poems," because they seem to be so true about the way of the world. Poets have been particularly unfortunate in securing plenty and pleasure in life, yet when the shadows of death and time have enveloped their frail forms, monuments in marble and bronze lift their artistic heads to tell the world of the fame of those that sleep below. Homer, Dante, Tasso, Otway, Goldsmith, Sheridan, Burns, Keats, Edgar Allan Poe, and Payne might rise from their graves today and view with wonder and alarm the great glory they secured after death as a contrast to the neglect and poverty they endured in life.

Many great and good soldiers sleep their last sleep on Arlington Heights, that we see in the glimmering distance. The dashing Sheridan, the gallant Crook, the great Indian fighter Harney, the faithful Quartermaster General Meigs, the Chief of Artillery Hunt, the Secretary of War Belknap, and the heroic Hazen, Sturgis, Ayers, Baxter, Crane, and the illustrious Admiral Porter, with a gallant crew of his naval subordinates, rest under the shadows of those grand old oaks.

More than 17,000 men who fought for the perpetuity of the

Union slumber in the field of eternal silence that once echoed to the footsteps of Gen. Robert E. Lee as he pondered amid the bowers of his ancestral home. Just outside the Government inclosure, to the north you find another " God's acre " filled with thousands of the sons of the South who fought and fell for what they, no doubt, deemed the right.

> " These in the robings of glory
> Those in the gloom of defeat,
> All with the battle-blood gory,
> In the dusk of eternity meet.
> Under the dust and the dew,
> Waiting the judgment day;
> Under the laurel, the blue;
> Under the willow, the gray."

Lengthen the view from where we now stand, at the Soldiers' Home, you behold fifteen miles away the hill tops of Mount Vernon, looming up in the fading horizon, and nearer, the walls of Fort Washington shining in the distance; the spires and smoke of Alexandria rising over the town where Jackson shot Ellsworth in his hotel, and where Brownell sent a bullet through the heart of the rash Virginian, who defied a whole Government, and flung his rebel flag to the breeze. Letting the eye linger along the banks of the Potomac you behold a long, dark line spanning its flashing waters, and you may see and hear the rapid railroad trains as they rumble over the crumbling timbers of the historic Long Bridge. Could this bridge talk, what a story it would tell of the hopes and fears of those beaten Union soldiers who crossed its piers in July, 1861, while the echo of cannon from Bull Run hastened their march from the field of battle to the Capital and the North.

> Bands were playing, horses neighing,
> Soldiers straying, mules were braying;
> Banners flying, women crying;
> Hearts were sighing, many dying;
> Onward, backward, all uproarious,
> The gray victorious, the blue still glorious;

> The field was won, the field was lost,
> Like ocean billows torn and tossed,
> And on the bloody field of war
> Were waves of dead, a giant scar,
> And mangled bodies, torn and pale,
> Like forests in a withering gale.

But, while the Union flag went down in the gloom of defeat at Bull Run, it rose triumphant at Gettysburg and Appomattox, and today the men who fought each other to the verge of death have shaken hands over the bloody chasm, and from yonder shining dome that tops the Capitol, right under the shadow of the Goddess of Liberty, they walk arm in arm to irrigate their anatomy with "cold tea" or exhilarate their manhood with rare wines and terrapin at the fine dinners of the Press, Gridiron, or Army and Navy Clubs, as well as the rare viands served up at the Arlington, Welcker's, and Chamberlin's. Thus, you see, the lamb and the lion can lie down together when the pasture is large enough to feed them both.

In these glinting remarks we must not forget to keep the grand panorama of Washington in view. There she sits, like an Egyptian Queen surrounded by the jewels of the Orient. At her feet flows the placid Potomac, winding like a silver serpent to the sea, while a rim of broken, emerald hills to the north sets off the opal and ruby colors that shine from the private and public buildings of this city of Magnificent Distances.

The swelling dome of the Capitol, the great marble monumental pile, 555 feet high, erected to the memory of the Father of his Country, and the War Department building, are the most prominent landmarks that meet the vision, while squares, parks, circles, angles, and long-shaded avenues fill the soul of the beholder with pleasure and pride as he contemplates the possibilities of Washington a thousand years hence, when the bright flag of the great Republic may irradiate the pathway of mankind and guarantee universal suffrage and home rule to the whole world.

A thousand years, my own Columbia,
A thousand years to rule the right;
A thousand years of law and order,
A thousand years of mind and might.

Poetry, painting, sculpture, music, and science cling to the skirts of the Goddess of Liberty, and, while with one hand she wields the sword of freedom, she may trample under foot the tottering thrones of tyrants and smash the lazaroni of royalty, who live on the sweat, the tears, and the blood of their fellowmen.

This Capital is the home of progress and the front-parlor compartments of 70,000,000 of free people. This is the altar in the cathedral of the continent, around which kneel the sons and daughters of Revolutionary sires, who wrung from monarchy the God-given principles of self-government. Here can be found men and women from every State in the Union and lingering travelers from every land under the sun, all mingling in social cheer or delivering into the arts and sciences which beautify life and increase the sum of human knowledge.

In the last twenty years untold millions of dollars have been invested in and around the city by public appropriations or private speculation. Waste lots and lands that a few years since would not bring 10 cents a foot cannot now be bought for $10 a foot, and old manor-houses that were ruined by time and war have been rebuilt or torn away to make room for the palatial mansions of rich citizens from Boston, Chicago, St. Louis, Philadelphia, Pittsburg, Cincinnati, or New York. And still the flood of capital, talent, and power rolls through our thousand gates, open night and day for the entrance and exit of mankind. The walls of Babylon, Thebes, and Rome do not hedge us in, and ancient barriers to the progress of man do not lift their cold, stony brows to beat back civilization.

Many statues of warriors and statesmen decorate the parks and circles of the city, and in a few years the number of illustrious men whose forms will appear in marble or bronze will exceed that of any other capital. They will not be complete, however, until that of Alexander Shepherd is erected in the most conspicuous spot in the city, for it was through his bold and far-seeing genius that we were lifted out of the mud and dust of slavery and placed in the concrete of freedom!

Aurora rising out of the blue Atlantic in her golden chariot smiles on this Paris of America as with rosy fingers she scatters the silver dewdrops of life and wealth along national pathways until she anchors her shining car beyond the golden sands of the Pacific!

> Age after age will sweep its course away,
> The works of man will crumble and decay,
> Yet on the tide of time from sun to sun
> Shall shine the glory of this Washington;
> And all the stars that in their orbits roll,
> Around the rushing world from pole to pole,
> Shall keep our name as true and bright
> As yonder sparkling jewels of the night.

CHAPTER XVII.

THE BATTLE OF SHILOH.

THE roar of the wicked gunboats, Tyler and Lexington, and the rumble of field-pieces broke upon our ears like a sad requiem over the graves of buried heroes. Bomb, bomb, thrumb, thrumb, sounded the music of our march, and through that long Sunday night the incessant song of the murderous gunboats was the death-knell of many a son of the South. The flood-gates of Heaven seemed open that fearful night, and the rain came down on the wearied trudging soldiers like hail-stones.

The roads were worked into sticky slush by the artillery wagons, and the weary warriors wound along amid peals of thunder and flashes of lightning, looking like gnomes from some infernal region. It was a hitch and a halt, a push and a run, a rest and a rout, until the straggling shanties of Savannah came into view on the swollen waters of the Tennessee, just as the gray of morning dissipated the black shadows of night and brought another day of battle and blood.

In passing through the streets of Savannah down to the transport steamer that was to take us to the battlefield, six miles above, I saw for the first time wounded soldiers borne on stretchers from the bloody work at the front. An hour before, the proud form of the soldier had been rushing on the enemy with the spirit of a lion; but now his mangled manhood lay prostrate, carried to the rear by sorrowing comrades, never again, perhaps, to mingle his voice with the roar of battle, sing love songs around the nightly bivouac, or greet the loved ones at home.

The Twenty-fourth Kentucky was immediately pushed aboard the transport steamer Evansville, and at once proceeded to the battlefield, arriving on the scene of slaughter and demoralization at noon. The Fifty-seventh Indiana and Twenty-fourth Kentucky were immediately placed in line of battle by Col. G. D. Wagner, commanding the Twenty-first Brigade, while the Fifteenth and Fortieth Indiana supported the advancing column.

The battle was raging, and the enemy was making a last stand on the rough hills behind a clump of water oak; and thick hickory underbrush, when amid shot, shell, and deadly buck and ball, Col. Lewis B. Grigsby, the commander of the Twenty-fourth, made the following impromptu speech as my regiment rushed to battle :

Fellow-soldiers, the field of honor is before you. The foe is over the hill waiting your salute. Kentucky looks to her soldiers to carry the flag of the Union to victory. Remember that you are sons of the heroic men who fell at the River Raisin, New Orleans, and on the bloody plains of Buena Vista. Stand by your colors to the last, preferring death to defeat. Now, at the enemy! Forward, guide right, charge!

The Fifty-seventh Indiana had dashed off to the front by this time, touching on the left of Rosseau's Brigade of Kentuckians, of McCook's Division; while the Twenty-fourth aligned on the left of the gallant Indianians, all charging right into the retreating forces of Van Dorn and Breckinridge, who moved with a sullen tread from their victorious ground on the previous day.

About a quarter of a mile to the left of Shiloh church, and near the Corinth road, the Twenty-fourth, in one of its charges, captured about forty prisoners and sent them to the rear. Among the prisoners were a field officer, a chaplain, and a surgeon named Redwood, of an Alabama regiment.

During the afternoon the closing battle scenes shifted with alternate success and defeat, the enemy contesting every inch of ground. But the army of General Buell, commanded by Nelson, McCook, Crittenden, and Wood, was too much for the heroic warriors of Johnston and Beauregard. About 4 o'clock the enemy was in full retreat, on the road and through the interminable forests leading to Corinth. Wood's Division followed the retreating army about five miles out on the Corinth road, and successfully repelled several cavalry dashes made by General Forrest; although in one instance the Confederate general dashed right through the Seventy-seventh Ohio Infantry as if it had been but so much chaff, scattering the blue-coats through the underbrush and tall timbers.

The darkness of night put an end to the bloody battle; and, after throwing out pickets on the various roads, Wood's division marched back to the main body of the army.

The armies of Grant and Buell slept upon the battlefield that soaking Monday night. No effort was made to follow the retreating foe. We were only too glad to rest after the terrible two days of blood and gather up the remnant of our broken forces.

" Our bugles sang truce, for the night-clouds had lowered,
  And the sentinel set their watch in the sky;
  And thousands had sunk on the ground overpowered—
  The weary to sleep, and the wounded to die."

Such a scene of havoc and desolation as the field of Shiloh presented I never witnessed in 'the marches and fights of after years. Around the old Shiloh meeting-house could be seen clumps of dead soldiers, scores of dead horses, broken artillery caissons, smashed wagons, tents riddled with bullets, trees torn to splinters, underbrush cut down by the murderous Minnies, great giant oaks blown up by the roots, and prostrate like the swollen human forms that festered below; while a look above presented the broken arms of the forest as they moved in the chilling night winds against the gloomy outline of a leaden sky!

The rain came down in torrents, the mud and forest slush being almost knee-deep. During the night I was detailed to take charge of the prisoners that we had captured in the afternoon. They were collected in a group under the dripping leaves and branches of a spreading oak. The night was chilly, the soldiers thin clad, and the demon of hunger threatened the weary warriors. In the race of Buell to the battlefield, commissary and regimental wagons had been left behind, and thousands of human beings were without shelter, save such temporary covering as could be obtained by broken branches, swamp grass, and long slabs of bark peeled from surrounding trees.

About 12 o'clock Monday night I was taken with a congestive chill and relieved from duty by Goodpaster, my companion lieutenant of Company I. In searching for shelter from the drenching rain and cutting winds, I stumbled into a tent that had been riddled by bullets, and feeling about in the midnight darkness, found some sleeping soldiers. In my wild hunt for rest I sank down between the sleepers, pulling their rough blankets over my shivering frame. Weary, cold, and hungry, I soon fell into a deep slumber, and on the airy wings of blissful dreams, was wafted away over hill, river, and plain to my home in Kentucky. I sat again by the fireside of those I loved, and basked in the sunshine of bright beauty. How my wild, delirious fancy painted happiness in the beautiful land of slumber and imagination. Angel voices lulled me to repose, rare viands and rich food haunted my hungry eyes, and sweet music cheered my sinking soul. The chill and pain of the midnight hour vanished away, the cold gray shadows of morning brightened the dark woods, when some straggling comrade roused me from the fantastic flowers and melodies of dreamland. The heart would fain slumber and the chill of the body beat back the sweet voices that implored me to linger in the realm of fancy.

"' Stay, stay with us; thou art weary and worn;'
 And fain was their war-broken soldier to stay;
 But sorrow returned with the dawning of morn,
 And the voice in my dreaming ear melted away."

Sorrow indeed returned; for, in rousing from sleep, I discovered that my blanket companions were dead, having been shot, no doubt, that terrible Sunday morning, when Sidney

Johnston and his dashing heroes rolled over the Union troops like mad waves on the sea-shore. At the door of the Sibley tent I saw dead soldiers scattered about like huge cord-wood sticks. In each of the company streets tattered tents, camp kettles, pans, broken guns, torn blankets, empty canteens, haversacks, and knapsacks lined the bloody battle ground. The "blue" and "gray" rested side by side in eternal sleep. Many I saw were grappled in death, and the bright bayonet that did the desperate work was clinched in the hand that dealt the murderous blow.

No mind can conceive or pen portray the startling horrors of Shiloh. It was, for the number engaged, the bloodiest battle of the war, and the very pivot of the victorious Union. Had Grant, Buell, and Sherman been defeated at Shiloh the Federal forces could not have been re-formed for battle south of the Ohio River; and Kentucky and Tennessee, in all human probability, would have been lost to the Union.

At 7 o'clock on the 6th of April, 1862, the division of General Sherman occupied the advanced position of the Union Army, his right rest on the Purdy road, near Owl Creek, and his left stretching in front and beyond Shiloh church on the Corinth road.

The division of Prentiss was on the left of Sherman, and McClernand occupied the line in rear of Sherman, while Hurlbut and Stuart were farther to the left rear, near the Tennessee River, leaving Lew. Wallace, with his lost division, in the swamps of Snake Creek.

General Sherman's division stood the brunt of the first day's battle, the desperate onslaught of Johnston bearing down on his left, and on the right of Prentiss, with the weight of a roaring flood, compelling the first line to fall back on McClernand for support, which was given promptly. General Prentiss and quite a large number of his division were taken prisoners in the morning, and during the subsequent fighting his command was but a shattered body staggering about on the bloody field.

Night found the Union forces badly demoralized, their left resting on the Tennessee River, having been driven from three battle-lines during the day. McClernand's and Sherman's divisions still occupied the ragged front of battle, while the victorious Confederates feasted on the provender of the Federal troops.

During Sunday night the gunboats Tyler and Lexington kept up a periodical fire on the enemy, throwing shells into the ranks of the victors. Grant and Buell had a consultation with their subordinates on Sunday night, wherein it was determined to take the offensive on Monday, and retrieve our lost ground, if possible.

Lew. Wallace occupied the extreme right of the Union forces, with Sherman, McClernand, Hurlbut, McCook, Wood, Crittenden and Nelson extending for two miles to the left, making a cordon of determined bayonets ready to pierce the enemy. They moved against the Confederate forces in unexpected strength early Monday morning; and, while varying success characterized the contending armies during the second day of the great battle, 4 o'clock in the afternoon found the rebel warriors in full retreat, and the Union army completely victorious.

I am satisfied that the Army of the Ohio, commanded by General Buell, turned defeat into victory, and were it not for the timely arrival of six divisions, the brave soldiers of Grant and Sherman would have been driven into the Tennessee River or captured by the daring soldiers of Johnston and Beauregard.

General Sherman, in his Shiloh report, says that Rousseau's brigade of McCook's division advanced beautifully, deployed, and entered the dreaded wood, where a few moments before Willich suffered defeat. He says: "I saw for the first time the well-ordered and compact columns of General Buell's Kentucky forces, whose soldierly movements at once gave confidence to our newer and less disciplined men."

Whole Union regiments from Ohio, Indiana, Illinois, Michigan, Missouri, and Kentucky were literally used up, and it was days and weeks after the battle before some Ohio regiments could be found, to form a nucleus for reorganization.

Perhaps it has never occurred to the peaceful citizen of today how much he is indebted to Grant, Sherman, Meade, Sheridan, Thomas, McPherson, Hancock, and other gallant commanders, for the blessings that came with the salvation of the Union and the starry flag. We think of these men, little realizing that to their brain, nerve, dash, and valor is largely due the establishment of a Union without a slave and a nation without a peer. They will only be entirely appreciated after their death, when their scurrilous detractors are rotting in unremembered graves. Their statues, in marble and bronze, will decorate the parks of the National Capital, telling to generations yet unborn the glowing history of their heroic actions at Donelson, Shiloh, Gettysburg, Winchester, Atlanta, and Appomattox.

Our forces held the field of Shiloh, but that was all; and, while the enemy leisurely retreated to Corinth, the victorious army showed no disposition to follow, but wallowed along like a huge anaconda for seven weeks, through the swamps and and forests of Tishimingo County, before reaching Corinth, only thirty miles away. General Halleck was preparing for a great battle with his 100,000 fresh soldiers, and when he actually got ready to strike the blow against Beauregard on the 30th of May, 1862, found that the heroic Confederate had evacuated Corinth with his entire army two days before, leaving nothing to our grand parade General but long lines of empty breastworks, broken camp kettles, and a few ragged prisoners!

It was laughable to see the preparations General Halleck made for the great impending battle which was to come off at Corinth. Rows of hospital tents, to accommodate a thousand men, were erected along the Purdy, Farmington, and Corinth roads; nice new cots, furnished with clean linen sheets; rose blankets; variegated quilts, and pillows with frilled cases, had been sent from the North to comfort would-be wounded warriors.

When long rifle-pits were dug every mile or so through the

woods the "boys" would say that they were all owing to the great forethought of General Halleck, who not only fixed up beds and shelter for the living, but provided new-made graves for the dead! The old General did everything in tip-top style, according to his "elements of war," except—fighting! This necessary element of war seemed to be a secondary consideration with the great tactician. Yet, at that time the war was young, and the Generals had to grow to the idea that the enemy had to be conquered, not by kindness, but by killing.

LOUISVILLE EXPERIENCE.

Many funny and curious scenes transpired about the camp, and in the homes of the rushing city. I became acquainted with a very beautiful Southern belle, whose family was of the best blood in the State. She had two brothers in the Army— one with Morgan, fighting for the "Stars and Bars," and the other with Rosecrans, fighting for the "Stars and Stripes." The father was old, and bowed down with grief at the terrible scenes transpiring around him, while the mother's mild manner sent a glow of love and peace through the household.

A social party was given at the mansion one evening, and I was invited to attend. On my arrival I found a large number of well-dressed guests, gray colors predominating, I being the only blue-uniformed individual present. Dancing, song, and feasting were indulged in until midnight, when, to cap the climax, Miss Ella asked the privilege of singing and playing the "Bonnie Blue Flag." As the tune had been filched from Yankeeland, and as I had heard "Dixie," another Yankee air, played in the heat of battle—and more particularly as I was not fighting against women and children—I interposed no objection. The beautiful young lady threw all her soul into the so-called rebel air, and out in the midnight silence it sounded as if the belles of Richmond were in chorus with the whole Confederacy. Great applause greeted the performance, but the cheers had not died away when a provost-martial with a squad of soldiers broke in upon the festivities and arrested the whole party for treasonable conduct. Everybody became alarmed at the predicament, the proprietor of the house seeing nothing but Camp Chase or Fort Lafayette, with their ponderous jaws ready to receive him.

In this emergency I replied to the arrest and taunts of the bluff captain, saying that I alone was responsible for the singing of the treasonable song, having requested the young lady to render the air for the social pleasure of the guests. He replied that if that was the case I should go with him at once to headquarters, where my conduct would be reported; and, as I took the responsibility of the song, I should suffer whatever penalty might be inflicted by the Government.

I bade the host and hostess good night, leaving them to their liberty and cheer, thus sacrificing myself for the good of other mortals. When I reached the commanding officer, who had authority and common sense, I explained that it was all a piece of fun and pleasantry and a magnanimous thought on my part to gratify an enthusiastic girl who desired to sing a few notes in honor of the Southern cause. The Confederacy always received my blows on the field of battle, but in the gloom of defeat I extended my hand and the generous words of a soldier to a fallen foe. I was not in favor of a parlor war, only striking those with arms in their hands.

The next day I called at the mansion and relieved the anxiety of the household by informing them that the commanding officer of Louisville had released me from arrest, while the superserviceable officer received no encomiums for his great energy and intense loyalty in breaking into a private house to disturb innocent festivities.

A few nights after this occurrence I stumbled on one still more ridiculous. Captain Gill, Lieutenant McIntyre, and myself had been at the Louisville Theater to see Maggie Mitchell in her charming play of "Fanchon." Before returning to camp, after the close of the performance, I proposed that we go to Walker's restaurant for refreshments. This proposition was readily agreed to, and without delay we repaired to the festive resort and ordered a fine bird supper. The small rooms, fitted for four persons, were well patronized that night, and the thin sheeting partitions could not shut out the voices or words of the respective occupants. During the supper a friend of McIntyre joined him—a citizen from the "blue-grass" region—who got into an argument with "Mac." on the proprieties of the war.

Champagne went down, and loud words quickly came up, until at last McIntyre made a lunge at the friend of his youth, knocked him against the panels of the small room, and down with a crash went the whole side on the elaborate supper of Maj. Gen. Gordon Granger and his staff officers. Excitement ran high, aad Granger's face looked like a thunder cloud that had been split up by lightning. He knew me, but did not know my companions. The suppers were destroyed. McIntyre and the citizen were finally separated, the lights turned out, and we were ordered to our camps under arrest, to report at the Galt House the next morning at 10 o'clock.

Granger and his officers were very jolly that night before we threw down the side of the stall on their supper, and I am convinced that our superiors were as much influenced by fumes from Bacchus as we were.

It was about 2 o'clock when we got into the street; and while we had been peremptorily ordered to camp, three miles away, and in a keen, frosty night, I proposed that, as we had to report to Granger at 10 o'clock in the morning, we go to the hotel, take a good rest and breakfast, and face the military music like men, which proposition was adopted.

Promptly at the appointed hour we put in an appearance at the Galt House. Granger was not yet out of bed. We told his orderly our mission, and asked him to inform the General. While waiting, it was agreed that I should do the talking and pleading, and that "the boys" should assent to every excuse I made for our conduct of the previous night. We were soon admitted, and found Granger sitting up in bed with his legs dangling over the side. We saluted, as became good, respectful officers, and he said: "Young men, you were drunk last night. I am ashamed and astonished to see officers of the Army conduct themselves in such a disgraceful manner."

I replied that we never drank, and before we left home we had each made a solemn pledge to our sweethearts that for the period of three years, or during the war, we would not taste, smell, or handle ardent spirits.

Granger looked astonished, and asked Gill and McIntyre if my statement was true. They held up their hands in earnest asseveration, and testified firmly to the truth of what I had uttered. The General arose immediately from the bed, proceeded to the mantel-piece, took therefrom a half-filled bottle of Bourbon whisky and glasses, and said: "Gentlemen, you are the most magnificent liars it has ever been my lot to behold. Your coolness and audacity deserve a reward, and I shall take it as a great favor if you will condescend to join me in a glass of old Bourbon."

I replied that his request was equal to an order; and, as we had sworn to obey all orders of our superior officers, the pledge we gave our sweethearts must give way to the rules of war; and however reluctant we might be to violate the obligations of love, we could not, with self-respect, decline to comply with the promptings of patriotism and duty.

We parted with mutual respect for each other. I believe that the General who takes a social glass with his staff is no worse than the soldier who empties a canteen with his comrade on the hot and dusty march. I shall never forget the Pickwickian look and quizzical smile of Granger on that occasion. He was certainly a generous character, and had the philosophy and common sense not to rebuke too severely the conduct in another which characterized himself.

> "The hand and heart will show the noble mind;
> A fellow feeling makes us wondrous kind."

CHAPTER XVIII.

BURNSIDE IN EAST TENNESSEE.

IN AUGUST, 1863, the Government determined to break one of the joints of the backbone of the Southern Confederacy by cutting loose from its base line in Kentucky, and moving by the way of Chattanooga and over the Cumberland Mountains to Knoxville, East Tennessee, where a grand trunk railroad that supplied men and material to the enemy might be cut, and force them to move their base line further to the south and the sea.

On the 23d of August, 1863, Gen. Ambrose E. Burnside, commanding the Department of the Ohio, and the Ninth Army Corps crossed the Cumberland River at the Somerset Ford with cavalry, infantry, and artillery, amounting to about 25,000 men. It was a bold strike to rescue East Tennessee from the Confederate foe. Before us laid a wilderness of more than 350 miles, with its mountain steeps, gorges, and streams.

The passage of the Cumberland at Smith's Ferry was a very difficult undertaking. On the south side of the rapid stream we were compelled to haul up the wagons and artillery with ropes grasped in the hands of a thousand men. When the army was safely camped on the south side of the Cumberland we rested but for one day, and then began a weary march through an unknown country that had been occupied by guerilla and regular troops of the enemy since the beginning of hostilities. A trail of twelve days through rugged mountains lay before us ere we could tap the East Tennessee railroad, near Knoxville, and sever Confederate communication from Richmond to the Southwest. Our wagon trains did not get up on the night of the 23d until 12 o'clock, and the soldiers had to camp on the bare, rocky earth, with nothing to cover them but overhanging branches, and no light to show them to dreamland but the twinkling stars peering out of the mysterious depths of the upper blue. The air was chilly and the sparkling jewels of Heaven shone down on the slumbering camp with a cold gleam. Early in the morning twilight, after a can of coffee, some raw bacon, and hard-tack, the whole army proceeded on a rough march to a small town named Jacksburg, traveling over narrow, rocky roads, that almost defied the passage of mules and wagons. We soon began to rise over the spurs of the Cumberland Mountains, winding our way across a back-bone ridge, until we came to the rapid waters of New River. The view at some high turning point in the road was grand and imposing, and in the clear morning air we could see at least a hundred miles away the undulating lines of the mountains sweeping away in graceful grandeur to the fading lines of the blue horizon.

In many instances we passed along a region for twenty or twenty-five miles without seeing a living sign of human habitation, and the tumble-down log huts and burnt chimney sites that we beheld convinced our minds that loyal hearts that once beat responsive to the Union were dead or refugees in Northern lands, far away from the glowing peaks and leaping streams of Tennessee.

On the 29th and 30th of August we passed over the topmost peak of the Cumberland Mountains and camped some ten miles from the town of Montgomery, situated near the southern base of the mountain range. The sight from the top of the mountain was most inspiring to the soul of man. Bold, bare rocks shot out against the clear sky like mammoth ships upon a raging sea. Deep, dark chasms yawned in majestic horror upon the eye of the traveler, and the thundering roar of some far-off falls broke upon the ear like the rush of mighty wind sweeping over a primeval forest. The mountain looks magnificent—

"Its uplands sloping decked the mountain side,
Woods over woods, in gay theatric pride."

Yet, to the romantic soul filled with unutterable admiration, the gloaming, the starlight, and the moonlight must intermingle to bring out in bold relief the beauty and grandeur of mountain scenery. A moonlight night I stood upon one of the wildest peaks of the Cumberland, the sighing pines singing to the stars, the wood crickets chirping at my feet, and the sounds of dashing casades carried on the wings and dreams of night, while the "bright and burning blazonry of God" glittered in their eternal depths and lit up the green mountain with a glow of celestial light.

At such a moment the soul communes with its Creator, and while we may, perhaps, doubt the reason of prayers, creeds, and churches, the most reasoning man cannot deny the existence of a God in the vast and mysterious realm spread out before him in air, water, earth, and sky. Those majestic mountain tops were not called into being and clothed with a rich eternal verdure by chance. Those crystal springs and roaring rivers did not rise and meander to the sea without some grand design. The blue heavens above were not spread out in illimitable beauty and dotted all over with shining worlds without a plan. No! God lives in every breeze that wafts over the earth; shines in every star that glitters in the blue vault of Heaven; sings with every warbler that flutters in the forest; breathes in every fragrant flower, and when the mortals of this transient life have lived out their small span they mingle again, for some unknown purpose, with the component parts of earth and sink back to some grand Omnipotence, wise and eternal!

Burnside and his troops passed through the city of Montgomery on the 1st of September, and while guerillas and rebel cavalry kept watch of our march from a safe distance, they did not, or could not, balk us in our grand design of cutting one of the main arteries of the roaring Rebellion. The dilapidation of the loyal town of Montgomery was sad to behold, and might well be compared to the Deserted Village of Goldsmith. Its inhabitants lived in rural comfort before the Rebellion, surrounded by smiling fields and productive vineyards that decked the upland, sunny slopes. These mountain people, sprinkled with a large colony of Germans, were true to the old flag when the tocsin of war was sounded, but were compelled to fly for their lives as refugees to the North. The plantation "chivalry" made it too hot for Union men to live in the atmosphere of slavery and and Confederate conscription. In going through the village I did not see a living citizen, but the torn roofs, broken fences, rotten doors, creaking sign-boards, straggling hedges, tall weeds, blowing thistles, hanging cobwebs, and "swallows twittering from their straw-built shed," betokened decay, desolation, and death.

> " Sweet, smiling village, loveliest of the lawn,
> Thy sports are fled and all thy charms withdrawn;
> Amidst thy bowers the tyrant's hand is seen,
> And desolation saddens all thy green.
> Sunk are thy bowers in shapeless ruin all,
> And the long grass o'ertops the mouldering wall,
> And trembling, shrinking from the spoiler's hand
> Far, far away thy children leave the land."

I left Montgomery and looked back with a sigh upon the straggling broken village just as the evening sun cast its last rays over the ruined homes of exiled, banished, loyal hearts, who forfeited all but truth and honor in their devotion to the Stars and Stripes.

After winding our dusty way for four days more we neared the railroad at Lenoir. The guerillas infested this region and became troublesome. At one spot, in passing a gorge in the mountain, at the Roaring Forks of the Holston River, three of the men of my regiment were killed by masked men in the brush. In the regiment were several fugitives or refugees from Tennessee. George Roburn knew every pass in the mountains and every ford along the streams. It was only the work of a moment for me to follow where the smoke of the guerillas' guns still scented the air. With Company I of the regiment I dashed after the mountain assassins and determined to wreak a sweet vengeance on the region that held such cut-throats. It was a perilous search, and somewhat like finding a needle in a haystack. We knew that to get on the south side the guerillas would be compelled to go to Campbell's Ford, and instead of going the easy, long path we cut right through the brush, into the scrub pines and cedars that blocked our way. Inside of an hour we arrived at the ford and secreted ourselves in the bushes to await results. About an hour before sunset we saw five men sneaking down the mountain side with long rifles on their shoulders. They were dressed in ragged butternut clothes, and might be the advance guards of Fra Diavolo's band of Italian robbers. They approached the stream very stealthily, sending one of their number to spy out the lay-off of the land. He finally blew a whistle that sounded like the shrill notes of a wild turkey, and in a few moments the gang of assassins were on the banks of the stream, ready to cross. My men were not a hundred yards from where they stood. I yelled out, "Halt!" They were startled for a moment, and then plunged into the rapid stream. One volley killed three of them, wounded one, and the other was washed ashore. I ordered the men to capture the wounded fellow and the captain of the band, whose name was Stafford. The wounded guerilla soon breathed his last, and Stafford threw himself on his knees and begged for mercy. He recited to me, with trembling, cowardly lips, that for two years he had been running away Union men from Tennessee, or forcing them into the Southern Army, and in many instances had killed these loyalists and burned down their homes.

We left "Captain" Stafford hanging to the limb of a sycamore tree with this placard hitched to his breathless bosom, "A robber, assassin, and spy."

It was long after night when we got back to the regiment, and was nearly daylight when we arrived in camp, after avenging the slaughter of three of my men.

The next day Burnside's army struck the East Tennessee railroad at Lenoir, proceeded to Concord, and on the 15th of

September, 1863, our loyal legions marched through the city of Knoville, and never let go our grip on that stronghold of mountain loyalty until the Rebellion gave its last kick at Appomattox. The story of the siege of Knoxville and our environment by Longstreet's troops has been told a hundred times. My regiment, the Twenty-fourth Kentucky, took a prominent part in the siege on the south side of the Holston River, and in my brigade were the One Hundred and Third and One Hundred and Fourth Ohio and Sixty-fifth Illinois, originally commanded by Daniel Cameron, of Chicago. A braver man I never met, and his regiment was composed of men as gallant and bold as ever marched, charged, or fell on the battlefields of liberty.

CHAPTER XIX.

JIM NELSON.

A TRUE TALE OF GEORGIA LOYALTY.

JIM NELSON was born in the mountains of northern Georgia, where, "from peak to peak, the rattling crags among, leaps the live thunder." When the Stars and Stripes were shot down at Sumter he was nineteen years old, tilling with his father a few famished acres of rugged, rooty, hilly land.

The sound of the shot at Sumter came rolling over the cotton plains until its echoes startled the loyal denizens of the mountains and convinced them of the fearful danger that beset their country. Those who favored rebellion and those who loved the Union took sides at once in heart or action. The neighbors of the lowland, who favored slavery, watched with a jealous and suspicious eye the action of the upland people, who almost invariably sided with the cause of liberty. Although these Georgia loyalists were greatly in the minority, the fact did not lessen their love for the Union or lessen their preparation for its defense.

Old Sam Nelson, the father of Jim, was a noted Unionist, and his mountain cabin soon became a rendezvous for hearts like his own. On the night of the 1st of June, 1861, seven of the loyal mountain men were gathered before the capacious chimney hearth of this fearless old Radical discussing the plan of raising a company to defend the old flag. The "back log" was long and high; hickory and oak were piled up in fantastic shape; the "dog irons" glowed in their effort to sustain the weight and heat of the leaping blazes as they sputtered, flashed, and roared up the wide, stick, sooty chimney.

The good housewife had spread a mountain meal of fried bacon, corn pone egg bread, hot biscuits, strong coffee, fried eggs, good butter, and milk; and, to cap the climax, there was placed at the head of the puncheon table a stone jug of the best "apple jack" in the county.

Sam Nelson had only two children, Jim and Katie, the latter two years younger than the boy. This pair that memorable night "passed the things around," while the "old lady" did the honors at the foot of the table, the "old man" sitting at the head dispensing food and fluid in equal quantities; perhaps more fluid than food.

When pleasure, peace, and patriotism, combined with song, pervaded the group of loyal hearts about the rustic board, a fiendish yell and loud rappings reverberated on the breeze, and in an instant the double room was filled with a score of masked, armed men. The leader made a sign, and in a period of less time than I can tell it the men were hustled out of the house, rushed into the woods nearby, and ignominiously shot—all save Jim Nelson, who rushed away into the darkness and hid himself in a secret cave that overlooked his childhood home.

The mother and daughter fled to a neighbor's cabin, three miles away, but ere they lost sight of their happy home they looked back through the midnight gloom and beheld the sky lit up with the burning sparks of their cabin. Jim, too, from his temporary hiding place saw sink into ashes the smouldering remains of all that was dear to him, and knew that but a few rods away his father and friends lay cold in death, while the chivalric (?) Confederates from the cotton fields below had vanished as quickly as they appeared, after a brilliant exploit of midnight murder and arson.

Then and there Jim Nelson swore in his heart and hissed it through his teeth that henceforth his life should be dedicated to wreaking vengeance upon any person or thing that aided the rebel cause. He alarmed his loyal neighbors early in the morning, and ere the sun was an hour high a group of friends had assembled about the dead patriots, and with a silent prayer of the heart they were wrapped in blankets and buried in one grave at the base of a pinnacled crag that overlooked the glimmering vale below. A dozen of the sons of the dead loyalists placed themselves at once under the leadership of Capt. Jim Nelson, and, armed with belts, bowie-knives, Kentucky rifles, and home-made ammunition, this desperate band, like the wild eagles of their native mountains, swooped down on their destined prey wherever found, and for three years were—a terror to regular, guerrilla, and citizen Confederates. Like Roderick Dhu's defiance to Fitzjames—

> "The mountaineer cast glance of pride
> Along old Lookout's living side;
> Then fixed his eye and sable brow
> Full on Fitz James: 'How say'st thee now?'
> These are old Georgia's warriors true,
> And Saxon—I am Roderick Dhu!"

The Confederate troops in large and various expeditions were sent into the Georgia mountains to blot out this daring band of patriots, but all effort proved unavailing, as the fox and tiger cat were not more skilled by nature in finding secret places of rest and security than Captain Nelson and his desperate comrades.

When General Sherman moved out from Tunnell Hill and through Snake Creek Gap, about the 6th of May, 1864, Jim and his little band heard the tramp of their Union brothers from the rugged heights of Rocky Face and Buzzard's Roost and followed in the wake of the conquering legions down to Resaca and Cartersville, on to the Etowah River.

While the army of Sherman was crossing the Etowah at Cartersville on pontoon bridges, the railroad bridge having been burned by the retreating troops of Johnston, Capt. Jim Nelson appeared at the headquarters of Gen. John M. Schofield, commanding the Twenty-third Army Corps, and disclosed a scheme to the General for burning and destroying the Confederate cannon and ammunition foundry, located about twenty-five miles above, on the headwaters of the Etowah. Jim knew every by-path, stream, rock, and hill in this iron region; and had but a short time before his appearance at Schofield's headquarters been employed as a mill hand at the foundry in question, where he, under the guise of a refugee from Kentucky, stored his mind with every detail surrounding the place, and when his daily labor ceased he would mingle with the regiment of Confederate cavalry that guarded the mill from their encampment at the south end of the rustic bridge that spanned the rapid, narrow stream. The shambling foundry was on the north side of the Etowah, abutting the broken bridge, and a mile below there was a country fording place.

All this and much more was told to the commander of the corps, communicated to General Sherman, and finally left to Gen. J. D. Cox to execute in his own way under the guidance of the mountain scout.

General Cox commanded the division that lay next to this duty. After a thorough talk with Captain Nelson he was finally introduced to Capt. James Caughlan, aide-de-camp on the staff of the General. He was ordered to select fifty men from the body of the division who would voluntarily join this forlorn hope in going within the enemy's lines for the purpose of destroying one of the material sinews of the crumbling Rebellion.

Captain Caughlan, a gallant young Irishman, soon selected from ten regiments—Reilley's and Cameron's brigades principally—the voluntary fifty men needed to destroy the munitions of the foe. As Caughlan was of my own regiment, and about my age, twenty-one, he asked me to be his second in command, and I consented with delight, for it has ever been my nature and ambition to think and act outside the mathematical ruts of mankind, and as " I set my life upon a cast, will stand the hazard of the die."

One bright morning, about the last of May, 1864, as the sun rose in splendor over the rugged hills of the Etowah, with two day's rations, forty rounds of ammunition for selected breachloading Winchester rifles, a single blanket, canteens, and light hearts, the fifty men, Captains Caughlan, Nelson, and myself left the beaten country road and plunged into the wild mountain paths of Georgia to do or die in the interest of Union and liberty.

About 5 o'clock in the afternoon we made a halt on a high hill about a mile from the object of our destruction. Through the towering trees and rolling hills we could see the smoke curl up into the clouds from the furnace and factory and hear occasional notes from the bugle of the cavalry as they sent out their evening calls, while the hum and roar of the mill died away as the supper hour of 6 o'clock released the workmen for the day.

We approached the mill by a secret path or ravine about 6:30, when the hands and cavalry guards were eating their evening meal in fancied security, and while the main body of our men were ambushed near the northern end of the bridge. Caughlan, the guide, and myself rapidly entered the factory, where hogsheads of turpentine were stored, and after laying prepared fuse in various places, even into the covered recesses of the ammunition room, we cast our lighted torches around the foundry, fired off the fuse, and ere five minutes had passed we were back with our men on a rapid retreat toward the hill we had left less than an hour before.

But on our rapid "advance to the rear" we had the glorious satisfaction to hear a continual discharge of shells and a sputter of cartridges as if a terrible battle was raging behind us, and then, too, as the rolling moon wheeled her nightly car into the warm summer sky, we beheld the smoke and flames of the burning building rise higher and higher, until the heavens were lit up with the consuming instruments of rebellion.

Loud and long we could hear the bugles and trumpets sounding " boots and saddle," as the " horse marines " of the Confederacy awoke to the realization that a " Yankee trick " had been played on their slumbering credulity.

For ten miles we kept on our course that lovely moonlight night, and when we thought that the chivalric cavalcade would not get to the ford below the burning bridge quick enough to intercept us before a safe distance from our lines, the guide, Captain Nelson, advised us to leave the woods and enter the main country road, where our progress would be easier and march more rapid. This we did, although very weary from the long march of the day and the excitement that a forlorn hope engenders.

We were leisurely winding our way up a long and narrow rocky hill, with steep sides, when all at once we heard the clattering sounds of the pursuing cavalry, like the far-off roar of falling waters. Something desperate must be done at once, and I suggested to Captain Caughlan that unless we gave the enemy the loads of lead in our breach-loaders we might never get to camp, or would at least stand a fine chance to become aristocratic boarders at Andersonville or Libby Prison. We halted at once just over the brow of the of the narrow summit and ordered the men to make a barricade of the fence rails that lined the road on each side, and also to tumble down such stones as lay loose on the steep banks. In less than ten minutes we had fashioned an impromptu fort that would have done credit to the most enthusiastic Frenchman when the guillotine was working off heroic heads in the streets of Paris.

It was understood that after we had pumped our loads of lead into the "bloods" of the Confederacy we were to again follow the guide, take to the woods, and never stop until we arrived inside the Union lines. We did not have long to wait. It must have been about 9 o'clock, and the moon shone as bright as day. Nearer and nearer came the roaring sound of the pursuing foe, while we lay close to the ground on our arms, ready to deliver the deadly volley at the order of our intrepid commander.

The jingling of swinging swords and sabers, the hoarse commands of officers, the labored snorts of horses, and the flash of their gleaming accoutrements as they rose over the brow of the hill, brought the command, "fire!" from our ranks, when all the front files of the foe went down in a heap, and as others followed, even to the pointed fence rails, we continued to fire down the narrow road until it seemed that a dark mass of men and horses filled the vacancy, making the night winds mournful with their dying groans. Bullets from the foe flew high and around us, but in a few moments all was comparatively still, while the "Yanks" had precipitately taken to the woods without the loss of a single man and only two slightly wounded—Jim Jackson and Tom Gill.

The first beams of morning lit up the gleaming tents of "Sherman's bummers," a mile away on the naked hills around Cartersville, and the shrill chorus of the thrilling reveille, as it resounded from regiment to regiment, echoed in our patriotic hearts like liquid tones of mellow music. We had performed our duty well, and as we drew up at a halt in front of Cox's headquarters and were dismissed to our various commands with rich compliments for our perilous labor, each man and officer felt as if the General of the Army was no better than himself.

Capt. Jim Nelson remained as a valuable scout around headquarters until the evacuation of Atlanta by Hood, where he was the first man that entered the city at the head of Slocum's corps, but as fate would have it, while he was investigating matters near the burning railroad depot, a bombshell exploded in his immediate front, inflicting a mortal wound, from which he died that memorable night. Yet, ere he breathed his last, he beheld the Stars and Stripes proudly floating over the capital city of his native State, and the murder of his father and friends was grandly avenged.

Capt. Jim Caughlan, my intimate friend, was killed at the battle of Franklin, Tenn., where Hood and the gallant Pat Cleburne, a Confederate Irishman, fought with desperation the victorious hosts of the Union. Caughlan and Cleburne were killed almost at the same time and place, one dying for the Stars and Stripes and the other for the Stars and Bars.

> "So, with an equal splendor
>   The morning sun rays fall,
> With a touch impartially tender,
>   On the blossoms blooming for all;
> Under the sod and the dew,
>   Waiting the judgment day,
> Bordering with gold the blue,
>   Mellowing with gold the gray!"

CHAPTER XX.

IOWA EXPERIENCE.

ON THE 1st of January I bid good-bye to the Twenty-fourth Kentucky never again to mingle with it in the rush of battle or join in its cheer of victory. Mountain, valley, stream, camp, and battlefield we left behind to many conrades who fell in the roaring fray; and while the birds sang as sweetly, the rivers ran as freely, and the flowers bloomed as brightly, they would never again awaken heroic melodies in the hearts of those daring warriors who went down in the shock and crash of battle.

To comrades who have the pangs of hospital treatment and the shock of war, I send forth greeting and say that while life lingers we cannot forget the glory and renown of the old Twenty-fourth, whose flag rose triumphant on many a battlefield and whose record for daring deeds may be equaled but cannot be surpassed by any regiment that served the Government.

The Twenty-fourth Kentucky was organized in the very face of treason. It defied relatives and friends for the sake of the Union, fought in front when loved ones at home were being destroyed by the enemy, skirmished on the advanced dead-lines of brigades, divisions, and corps as an entering wedge to victory, marched by road, rail, and boat more miles than any other regiment in the service, and at last furled forever the torn and blood-stained flag to rest with the archives of a State saved to the Union by its valor.

To every soldier in every land, and in every good cause, I extend a heart and hand, whether or not we kneel at the same altar or worship the same God.

Fame, like the soul, is immortal.

> "The stars shall fade away, the sun himself
> Grow dim with age, and nature sink in years;
> But thou shalt flourish in immortal youth,
> Unhurt amidst the war of elements,
> The wreck of matter, and the crash of worlds."

The unsettled state of society in my old Kentucky home induced me to accept an invitation to visit an uncle who lived in Allamakee County, Iowa.

The winter of 1865 was very severe in the Northwest. A few quite frigid days among the rugged, snow-capped hills of Allamakee made me wish for the warm rays of the sunny South and the genial smiles of those dear old army friends I left behind. I was about to leave the Hawkeye State in disgust at the cold reception nature extended, when my uncle and family suggested that I should procure a country school and turn my mind away from brooding over the past.

I concluded to make application for a school located at Paint-Rock Church, overlooking the waters of the Mississippi River and within a mile of Harper's Ferry, a small town in the southeastern part of the county.

The trustee of the school, Barry, was willing that I should enter upon the duties of teacher at once, but a certificate must first be procured from the county superintendent, whose office was located at Waukon, the county seat, fifteen miles away. I easily procured the needed certificate.

Being now armed with official authority, I presented myself at the new stone school-house one blue Monday morning in January, 1865, and began the role of a country pedagogue.

Arriving early in the morning from Harper's Ferry I unlocked the establishment and found nothing but cheerless walls, damp and musty. A few benches were scattered about the room, and a pine desk was stuck in one corner to accommodate the presiding autocrat. An old Franklin stove that might have warmed its namesake in the Revolutionary War opened its broad jaws for the reception of fuel. The wood-pile outside was unchopped. As some of the "big boys" gathered in, I advised them to procure an axe from one of the neighbors and split enough wood to dispel the cold and frost that had settled on the stone wall, and even fringed the "Old Franklin" with fantastic embellishments. After digging about in three feet of snow that surrounded the wood-pile and school-house, we finally fished out enough to make a roaring fire and warm the shivering children that vied with each other in scorching their clothes in an effort to straddle the stove.

When 9 o'clock arrived I rang the bell with the air of a successful auctioneer, keeping a stern face that would have done great credit to a philosopher of sixty, much more to a youth of twenty-two who had just launched out as an educator.

When silence prevailed I rose at the desk and addressed the seventy-five scholars who came from the snow-clad farms of Allamakee.

I merely said that I had been employed by the trustees to teach the school for a period of six months and hoped that the boys would behave like gentlemen and the girls act like ladies. In conclusion, I had only to lay down the simple rule that when they did right I should reward them, and when they did wrong I should certainly punish them.

These remarks were taken by the younger children with humility, but a few of the larger boys winked at each other, as much as to say, "That's an old gag; that can't frighten scholars who have ducked bigger teachers than you are. It might be well to give that speech to the 'marines,' but for the stalwart sons of Erin living among the grubs of Allamakee it will not do; the colors of your eloquence will not wash!" Notwithstanding this imagined reply to my first and last effort as a teacher, I proceeded at once to bring order out of chaos and to class the school.

The third day of my mission brought about a free fight among the scholars, during my absence at dinner. When school was called I proceeded to ascertain the cause of the row. It seems that a son of Erin and a waif from the Fatherland disputed about the honor and bravery of their ancestors, and the other scholars joined in the fight with a clannish spirit that would have been an honor to the bogs of Ireland or the upland slopes of Scotland. After due investigation, I implicated only seventeen boys and girls in the fight, sending the residue of my institution to their seats and books. When all was ready, I went to business with a fine hickory ruler that had been provided in anticipation of just such troubles. The smaller scholars took their light punishment with suppressed sobs, and went to their benches with sulks. The leader of the riot was the only one who attempted to resist and treat my proposal to whip him with contempt. I reasoned with the stalwart Hibernian, impressing upon him his violation of school rules and my intention to have equality of punishment. He finally squared off, swore with the swagger of a prize-fighter, but ere he could execute his threat I hit him with the rule just under the ear and sent him to the floor in a shiver of pain. A dipper of water brought him to, in tears, when I finished his punishment by additional blows on his hands, sending him to his seat as if nothing had occurred to disturb the equanimity of the school.

From that day to the close of my term in June I was boss of the institution, and had no further occasion to punish any of the scholars. When the examination and exhibition closed on the last day, scholars, parents, and friends left me with thanks, praise, and tears; and many of my dear old pupils will remember to this day the pleasant hours and loving chats we had under the noon-day shade of Paint-Rock Church and the delightful strolls we took among those rugged hills and blooming vales.

My experience as a village schoolmaster will long be remembered; and the beautiful site of the school, church, and graveyard was all that the most romantic and poetic heart could wish. Situated on a high hill, overlooking the rolling plains to the west, and commanding a view to the south and east, with the waters of the Mississippi sweeping along to the sea, it was no wonder that my young heart swelled with emotion when contemplating the beauty of the landscape. How often have I lingered in the tangled walks of the old churchyard, under a spreading oak, and gazed in rapture at the golden glory of the setting sun, as the storm clouds in the west swept across the cardinal colors of the day. My pathway through woods and fields was made radiant with boys and girls. Sleigh rides, parties, and occasional balls at Harper's Ferry intervened to banish the monotony of country life, and while I kept the face of a stern philosopher in the school-room, I acted with all the vanity and freedom of a drum-major in the ball-room.

Spelling matches at the country schools were occasions for fun and opportunities for the belles and beaux to indulge in the never-ceasing eccentricities of Cupid, who shoots his arrows where least expected, inflicting wounds that never heal and pleasant pangs that never die.

My patrons and scholars insisted that I should give a spelling match at the old school-house, and as I was always ready and willing to indulge the love of sociability, I readily consented to the proposition. The evening arrived, and with it came more than a hundred of the neighbors and their children, anxious to battle for the mastery in spelling, after which dancing was indulged in to the great satisfaction of all present.

A match was soon arranged by two rural beauties, who tossed up for the first choice of spellers. I was chosen by one of the contestants, and so it went on to the end of the programme, when two lines of warlike intellects stood facing each other for battle. The person who missed stepped down and out, and the one that remained on the floor to the last carried off the prize and became the noted champion of the evening. After the first round, a simple word was given to me by the umpire, and, ludicrous to relate, I went down at the first shot, retiring to one of the benches amid the laughter of the whole audience.

A beautiful young girl of fifteen carried off the prize, receiving the encomiums of the whole house for her remarkable memory and precise information. I know it is inexcusable for a man of education to be a bad speller; but, even to this day, I am liable to insult the memory of Noah Webster, and even rattle the bones of Lindley Murray, in violating his rule that a verb must agree with its nominative in number, person, and case.

The schoolmaster is a wonderful man among yeomanry, and the greatness of Goldsmith's pedagogue may well illustrate his rural renown:

> "The village all declared how much he knew,
> 'Twas certain he could write and cipher too;
> Lands he could measure, terms and tides presage,
> And even the story ran that he could gauge;
> In arguing, too, the parson owned his skill,
> For e'en though vanquished, he could argue still;
> While words of learned length and thundering sound
> Amazed the gazing rustics ranged around;
> And still they gazed, and still the wonder grew
> That one small head could carry all he knew."

At the conclusion of my school I went to Lansing, and through the instrumentality of the county treasurer, a shrewd and pleasant gentlemen, was employed to collect delinquent taxes, long due by the rustic citizens of Franklin and Linton townships. With the necessary books and a commission as deputy collector, I took up my headquarters at the village of Volney, and advertised that I was ready and willing to collect delinquent taxes. I waited for my pronunciamento to take effect, but as the good people did not rush frantically from the hills and valleys in response to my call, I concluded to go to the mountain, since the mountain would not come to me.

The life of a delinquent tax-collector is not a happy one—particularly where the ground has been worked over for ten years by ambitious deputies. The doctor is looked upon with fear and anxiety by his patient; the lawyer is tolerated with hope and suspicion by his client; the undertaker comes with a melancholy face to perform the last sad duty for mankind; but the delinquent tax-collector is looked upon in his official capacity as a combination of all the horrors—a pest to be avoided and a nuisance to be abated.

I spent the month of July, 1865, among the hills of Yellow River, coaxing and threatening the good people with penalties unless they paid the real and personal taxes demanded in the name of the Hawkeye State, and was unusually successful in securing the payment of taxes that had slumbered for many years. I shall never forget the bold move I made on an old Irish bachelor who lived like an anchorite on a forty-acre farm perched on a rugged height overlooking Yellow River. He owed the State of Iowa about $50, but had for more than ten years evaded every tax-collector who came to the neighborhood. They could never find him at home when endeavoring to give the notice of levy, and although the deputies often climbed the bluffs in pursuit of the delinquent, they never succeeded in getting the taxes.

Duly armed with my legal documents and an army "pepperbox," I started away one bright morning through the crooked defiles leading out from Volney, and began to climb the heights reaching to the lands of the fierce old bachelor. I imagined myself for awhile in the highlands of Scotland or among the heather mountains of Ireland, in search of some bold outlaws who worked the secrets of the still. While thus musing, in contemplation wild, I beheld a curl of smoke rising out of a clump of trees and saw a yoke of oxen grazing near a cornfield in the vicinity of the old bachelor's cabin. I let down a pair of bars, turned the cattle into the cornfield, and awaited developments. The joy of the cattle was great while crunching the young corn, and all went merry as a marriage-bell until the old bachelor rushed from his cabin, bareheaded, and yelling like a trooper at the oxen. The thought of saving his crop made him oblivious of my presence. As he rushed by me in his flight after the cattle, I cried, "Halt!" He looked at me with a gaze of astonishment, showing all the rage of a trapped lion. I at once made known my business, and with the legal documents in one hand and a revolver in the other, served due notice on the delinquent, levied on his yoke of oxen to satisfy the debt, and thus, with the air of a victorious General, maintained the majesty of the law and sustained the honor of Iowa, while threatening to blow off the head-piece of a citizen if he dared to decline my demand or interfere with me in the execution of my office.

When he realized the trap he had fallen into and saw me drive off his cattle, he immediately sued for quarter; and before I got back to Volney he had caught up with me and tendered the taxes with all penalties and costs attached. I gave the old fellow his receipt in full, released the oxen, shook his hand, bade him be virtuous and consequently happy; and I have no doubt but that the lesson he received gave him greater respect for human laws, and a wise discrimination to know that a legal document, backed up by a pistol, is not to be ignored.

My duties as a tax-gatherer soon ceased, and after deducting my per cent. I turned in the balance to the treasurer of Allamakee County.

*　　*　　*　　*　　*　　*　　*

I had often heard that it was sweet to die for one's country; and, as I was filled with hope and poetry, I concluded to cast my drag-net into the Republican county convention that assembled at Waukon on the 18th of August, 1865.

After a laborious campaign among the primary caucuses, making all the promises incident to a canvass of a Congressman, assuring the honest voters that they were the salt of the earth and I but the humble instrument to wait for and record their will, the convention met, and I received a unanimous vote as candidate for the legislature. As this high honor came unsought (?) to a man of twenty-two, who had lived in the county scarcely a year, I could do nothing else but accept in a modest (?) speech, expressing the usual surprise and informing the convention of my unworthiness; then soaring aloft in the realms of native eloquence, I pledged undying love to the principles of the Republican party and proposed to bear onward the standard of freedom until the election sunset of October shone pure and bright upon the victorious folds of the star-spangled banner planted upon the crumbling ramparts of Democracy!

I made a joint canvass with the Democratic nominee, who was more than fifty years of age—an old stager who could change his political opinions with as much ease and facility as a diver changes his suit.

SENATOR ALLISON.

I shall never forget the first time I met Col. William B. Allison. It was under rather peculiar circumstances, and in the month of September, 1865, at Waukon, Iowa, the county seat of Allamakee.

Governor Stone was running on the Republican ticket, and the State issue was an amendment striking the word "white" out of the Hawkeye constitution, so that the black man or any other man might have equal rights before the law in the State of Iowa.

At the time above mentioned Colonel Allison was making a Congressional canvass of the twelve counties in his district, and dropped in at Waukon the very evening that Paulk and myself were to enlighten the natives at the court-house. It was rather embarrassing for Allison, as Paulk did not wish to divide time with the Congressman, but I finally prevailed on him to let Allison have from 7:30 to 8 o'clock, and he could take another hour, while I would be satisfied with half an hour to close the debate.

The court-house was packed with ladies and gentlemen, and a large gang of Democratic "heelers," headed by Johnny Armstrong, the editor of the Lansing *Journal*, came a distance of twelve miles with the avowed purpose of preventing me from speaking, because of the previous "roastings" I had given Paulk and the "copperheads."

Mr. Allison began his speech in due time upon the State issues and the contemplated reconstruction laws that were about to be enacted in Congress. His remarks were calm, solid, and direct. Speaking of striking the word "white" out of the Constitution, he said, among other things:

The word "white" in our Constitution is now obselete, since the Emancipation Proclamation of President Lincoln knocked the shackles off four millions of slaves and lifted them into the sunlight of freedom. It is a relic of a tyrannical oligarchy, and should no more pollute or disgrace our fundamental legal instrument, but be swept away to the other rubbish piles of Democracy.

The slave of yesterday is the freeman of today, and he must and shall be protected by all the power of the General Government. Four millions of these recent bondsmen lift their hands and faces to us imploringly to take them out of the slough of slavery and ignorance and bear them up to the high plane of freedom. Shall we deny the wail and cry of humanity? No! Every mortal in this grand Nation must stand equal before the law, and the noble soldiers who bore our starry flag through many fierce and bloody battles will still see to it that every man shall be protected in his inalienable and God-given rights.

These were brave words at that time and place, and the black man, North or South, who shall ever prove recreant to the lofty Lincoln, the eloquent Phillips, the glorious Garrison, and the alert and persistent Allison deserves no memorial to mark his remains.

Mr. Paulk arose and attempted to reply to the Congressman, but his argument was about as strong as a bag of feathers let loose against a blizzard, while the phalanx of facts put forth by Mr. Allison remained unanswerable.

Turning around, the old gent accused me of being an interloper in Iowa, a "carpetbagger" from Kentucky, a beardless presumption, a boy without a residence, and nothing but my cheek to pay taxes upon!

After this broadside shot at the "subscriber," I rose to close the debate. I had found out a good many things against the record of this political hack. I pictured him as a sutler soldier, a "copperhead," "Knight of the Golden Circle," and a former carpetbagger from Vermont, who turned his coat when he migrated West for boodle, beans, and barley. In fact, I ripped him up the back in grand shape with all the satire and invective that a fellow "raised" in Kentucky might be expected to indulge in. My crowd cheered to the echo, but the Lansing "gang" hissed, yelled, and tried their best to howl me down, and persisted in breaking up the meeting, but Col. McAdams and Captain Granger, with a platoon of recently discharged soldiers, hustled the leaders of the riot out of the court-house, and old Paulk, their leader, followed in red-faced disgust, leaving me master of the situation and in charge of the fine audience.

Walking over to the hotel, after the meeting, Mr. Allison asked me how I could expect to be elected in a Democratic county of more than 300 majority. I replied that I did not expect to be elected, but to reduce the majority and pester and worry the "copperhead" heathens to the best of my ability; and I further remarked that the "doughfaces" of the North and "guerrillas" of the South had barely enough courage to linger in the rear and assassinate, but not enough to go the front and fight like gentlemen and soldiers, and the boys who wore the "blue" and those who wore the "gray" had an utter contempt for the "fire in the rear" phalanx, and mankind would always despise assassins.

Allison coincided with my impulsive statements and remarked: "What are you going to do after the election?" "I'm going to resume the study of law if I can find some lawyer to furnish me a desk and a split-bottom chair, with Blackstone, Kent, Chitty, Greenleaf, *et al*." He laughed, and said "Well, good-night; come down to Dubuque after you're counted out, and I'll try and find you a corner."

The day after the vote was announced, having lost all my enthusiasm in the election, I embarked on the fine steamer Gray Eagle, at Lansing, and proceeded to the city of Dubuque. Standing on the hurricane deck of the steamer as she swept away from the wharf, and rounded toward the bald bluff of

South Lansing, I breathed a sigh of regret at leaving relatives, pupils, and friends, where youth and love had mingled in the scene, and confidence and ambition cast a glow of supreme happiness through the halls of memory. Some very dear friends are yet living in Iowa, who may call to mind the scenes I have depicted; and, perhaps, in the evening twilight, when the walking shadows of night climb the river bluffs, they may recount to their children and friends the romantic career of a country pedagogue and would-be legislator.

Arriving in Dubuque, I called at the law office of Mr. Allison, the Congressman I met in the late canvass. I told him of my desire to continue the study of law, which had been interrupted by the war. He at once secured me a clerkship in the office of Henry A. Wiltz, the United States surveyor general for Iowa and Wisconsin, at the same time tendering the use of his books and office.

I spent the winter of 1866 and the summer and fall of the same year in the diligent study of the law, pondering on the wisdom of Blackstone, Chitty, Kent, Parsons, and Greenleaf, with all the enthusiasm of youth and ambition, receiving my license to practice as an attorney in the courts of Iowa on the 11th of November, 1866.

The memories that cluster about Dubuque can never be forgotten, and the friends that assisted me in the old Julian building in the study of law present themselves today in the form and appearance of yesterday.

Mr. George Crane and Capt. T. Palmer Rood were the law partners of Mr. Allison, and while he was mostly engrossed in political calculations, they attended strictly to the details and work of an important firm. Mr. Crane was a man of fine judgment, and had the entire confidence of his clients and the respect of the bar, which numbered some of the best lawyers in Iowa, such as Bissell, Shiras, Adams, Mulkern, Samuels, Knight, Wilson, Cram, Henderson, Cooley, O'Donnell, and a rare genius named Charles McKenzie.

Senator Allison was appointed a colonel on the staff of Governor Kirkwood soon after Fort Sumter was fired upon in the spring of 1861. He rendered invaluable services in enlisting, organizing, and equipping Iowa troops for the battlefield. His energy and patriotism went hand in hand night and day, until the Hawkeye State filled its quota, and gave to President Lincoln, for the defense of the Union, a corps of gallant soldiers that may have been equaled by some of their comrades, but never surpassed by any on the great battlefields of the Rebellion.

I have known Colonel Allison intimately for thirty years, and I can say, in all candor, that I never met a public man, and I met and knew many national characters, who could work so silently, patiently, and effectively as he has in all the varied and complicated duties that fell to his lot. Duty and work are his watchwords, with faith and friendship the main elements in his close-knit composition. Like the coral insect, he labors silently and incessantly, paying particular attention to details, and you never hear or see his work until it is complete.

As a financier he has no superior in the United States Congress. For years the impress of his financial genius has been ingrafted on the internal revenue and cusiom laws of the Nation through the Committee of Ways and Means of the House. For nearly eighteen years in the Senate, through the Finance and Appropriation Committees, he, with Morrell and Sherman, have been the wheel horses of practical financial legislation.

I say it without fear of contradiction, and his compeers I believe will agree with me, that Allison is the best all-around equipped man in the United Congress for go-ahead, practical, business, common sense, greenback, gold, and silver legislation. He never made a friend that he lost; and many a political foe has he turned into friendly accord. He never made a personal or political promise that he did not fulfill, sooner or later, and those who know him best love him most. He is modest, laborious, and shrewd, and has a very fine conception that this is a Nation with a great big N—where luxuries, internal and external, should be taxed liberally to defray the expenses of the Government, and taxes on the necessaries of life lightened as much as common sense and justice demands.

Allison is conservative, on general principles, but when you arouse him on a special point, where the interest of the Nation is at stake, he throws aside his velvet cloak and steps into the arena like a Roman gladiator and hurls javelins of radical logic at his opponents. He has innate pride without vanity, continuousness, without cringing, manhood without mediocraty and absolute bravery without any bravado. Around the social board he is the toast of his friends, as tender and kind as a woman and as forgiving as a philosopher. Like Grant, he is true to his friends, and once inside the circle of his confidence, no power on earth can alienate his heart or chill the sentiment of his soul for those he loves and admires.

ORATIONS.

I.

HECTOR.

[A Newfoundland Dog. Kentucky: 1857.]

MY DEAR SCHOOMATES: We come to praise and bury Hector. For many long years he has been our daily and nightly companion, sharing with us the sports of school and our truant rambles to "Conners' swimming hole," at the bend of the creek.

Hector was descended from an illustrious family of Newfoundland, where arctic winds, drifting snows, and floating ice fill up the measure of the fleeting year. He was stricken with pneumonia on Christmas Day, and peacefully passed away as the old year lapsed into the realm of shadows.

Spring, with her young wild flowers; Summer, with her red-ripe apples and blackberries; Autumn, with her forest nuts, and wild, old Winter, with his hoary locks, found Hector by our side, ready at all times to lead or protect us.

No contumely, sticks, stones, or abuse could chill the warmth of his morning greeting or the friendly wag of his expressive ears, nose, and tail. Although often rebuked and humiliated by our thoughtless conduct, he held a forgiving spirit and extended his great, black paw as a token of sincere reconciliation. We shared with him our lunches, and in moonlight hours, when we played "hide-and-seek," he led the town dogs in vociferous glee when we ran to touch the base!

At every frolic, fight, or fire, he was first on deck, and the town marshal often sought his aid to accelerate the movements of lazy, vagrant hogs that made the street their forage pasture and the sidewalk their sty.

On election day, when crowds of town and country revelers grew hilarious at the saloon or drugstore, Hector might be seen with dignified mien and sober countenance contemplating the the weakness and folly of lordly man, who got drunk and did not have as much sense as a dog! How often have we seen him with reins in his mouth, carrying on his back little Nellie Gray or Billy Bascom, and sometimes trotting before a cart to the delight of the rider and the admiration of the public. His master, the tavern keeper, and old Mose, the stable boy, will greatly miss their faithful watch-dog, but we boys will never again find such a friend.

Hector has passed away from the sorrows and shadows of life to the sunlight of a glorious death. His generous spirit reigns where suns and stars shine eternal, and where the cruel midgets of mankind cannot practice upon him their ingratitude. Hector had not time enough to be a hypocrite. He was simply an honest dog. He saw things direct without any of the trappings of deceit, rose before the dawn, held up his heart and head at high noon, and when the sun went down over the waters of Slate, he repaired to his quarters at the tavern like a decent dog and partook of such biscuits, beef, and bones as black Mose manipulated for his edification.

While Pharisees preached, Hector practiced what he felt, and the poorest person in rags could always command his society and depend on his protection. He was none of your stuck-up, parlor, dilletante dogs that needed an introduction before taking you into "their set." No, indeed; we knew him as an everyday dog, wearing his curly hair on his broad back as God had fashioned it, and giving his cheering voice to all our pleasures.

Hector had a clean conscience for a creed, and divine instinct for his rule of life. He was a rough ashler, cracked from the quarry of truth, and stood as a shining example to the dogs of the town, that regarded him as a leader in all their moonlight, midnight meetings, when holding canine conventions beneath the sparkling stars and magic moon. Hector was a good neighbor, a staunch friend, and never garnished his voice or deeds with the hideous harangues of hypocrisy or ingratitude.

Lord Byron's lines to his dog, "Boatswain," at the expense of mankind, might well be uttered over the remains of Hector.

> "When some proud son of man returns to earth,
> Unknown to glory, but upheld by birth,
> The sculptor's art exhausts the pomp of woe,
> And storied urns record who rests below;
> When all is done, upon the tomb is seen,
> Not what he was, but what he should have been;
> But the poor dog; in life the firmest friend,
> The first to welcome, foremost to defend,
> Whose honest heart is still his master's own,
> Who labors, fights, lives, breathes for him alone,
> Unhonored falls, unnoticed all his worth,
> Denied in Heaven the soul he held on earth;
> While man, vain insect, hopes to be forgiven,
> And claims himself a sole exclusive heaven.
> Oh, man! thou feeble tenant of an hour,
> Debased by slavery, or corrupt by power,
> Who knows thee well must quit thee with disgust,
> Degraded mass of animated dust!
> Thy love is lust, thy friendship all a cheat,
> Thy smiles hypocrisy, thy words deceit,
> By nature vile, ennobled but by name,
> Each kindred brute might bid thee blush for shame.
> Ye who perchance behold this simple urn,
> Pass on—it honors none you wish to mourn;
> To mark a friend's remains these stones arise,
> I never knew but one; and here he lies!"

II.

DECORATION DAY.

We stand upon the hilltop of patriotism to pay truthful tribute to the memory of our loyal dead.

Let us, the survivors of "grim-visaged war," renew our devotion to the great Republic and swear by the blood of our dear old comrades that the "Red, White, and Blue," under which they fought and died, shall symbolize forever—all freedom for all men!

Rebellion, with its horrible visage, has gone like the echo of a vanished dream, and its votaries are buried forever in the dark waters of oblivion, while that glorious flag for which our comrades fought, waves triumphant over a consolidated Nation.

The Union is absolutely secure, and no domestic or foreign foe shall ever again jeopordize the integrity of the Republic. The pines of Maine, the palmettoes of South Carolina, and the orange trees of California have made a tripartite bower over a united country that shall shelter and protect all the people as long as the Atlantic and Pacific, with their bounding billows, beat against our rock-bound shores.

The debt of gratitude due the battle warrior can never be fully liquidated. The Nation that forgets its soldiers and sailors should be erased from the face of the globe, and over its remains should settle the stagnant waters of oblivion.

The progress of the world has been carried forward on the point of the bayonet, and the flash of the soldier's sword has lit up the pathway of liberty and terrified the tools of tyranny.

Alexander, with fifty thousand men formed into the irresistable Macedonian phalanx, conquered a million of Persians at the battle of Arbela, overran the Oriental world, carrying the letters and architecture of immortal Greece into the very heart of Asia, making princes and potentates the playthings of his vaulting ambition and writing his name on the highest pinnacle of military splendor.

Monuments and cities arose in the track of his victorious army like waterspouts from a stormy ocean, and he seemed to wield the wand of the Magi and rub the lamp of Aladdin with the facility of a necromancer and universal genius, who never knew defeat until the sparkling wine of the Hercules cup sent his sighing soul to the realms of Pluto.

Cæser flashed into the Roman world like a brilliant meteor in a midnight sky, lighting up the pathway of the Empire with the flashing swords and lances of his loyal legions, that scaled the sky-kissing Alps, camped under the shadows of the pyramids, and carried his victorious eagles through the forests of Germany, Gaul, and Brittain.

And then turning his invincible legions on Rome, he crossed the Rubicon, marched triumphantly into the imperial city, routing Pompey and his senatorial compeers into Spain, Greece, and Egypt, until at last the head of his great rival was presented as a bloody offering to his towering ambition. As soldier, statesman, orator, historian, and poet he will be grandly mentioned down the rolling ages to the last syllable of recorded time, while Brutus and Cassius, his cowardly assassins, will be mentioned only to be execrated for their dastard perfidy and ingratitude.

Napoleon, the classic Corsican, has left his indelible footprints on the sands of time, and so long as Lodi, Austerlitz, Marengo, and the fatal Waterloo are remembered, this giant military and civic genius will be admired by millions of mankind.

He rises before us—

"Like some tall cliff that lifts its awful form;
Swells from the vale and midway leaves the storm;
Though 'round its breast the rolling clouds are spread—
Eternal sunshine settles on its head!"

And yet, Alexander, Cæser, and Napoleon fought for personal glory, conquest, and Empire, rearing a hecatomb of human bones as a bloody mount for their demoniac and insane ambition.

But, in our own God-given Republic, Washington, Jackson, and Grant fought for a Government of the people, by the people, and for the people.

Lincoln, by a single stroke of his inspired pen, erased the dark blot of slavery from the escutcheon of the Nation, freeing four millions of bondsmen, and yet, after all, it was the soldier Grant and his comrades that punctuated with his sword the strength and might of Lincoln's pen.

Here rest the grand warriors who swung the trip-hammer of battle that smashed the red-hot blazing bloom of the Confederacy, and knocked off forever the galling shackles of the slave. Here sleep the brilliant officers and brave men who sacrificed themselves on the bloody altar of their country and died for the principles of heaven-born freedom.

Here let us dedicate an everlasting temple to heroism. This green sward shall be a mausoleum of heroic hearts, its dome the bending heavens, and its altar candles the watching stars of God. Year after year let us assemble at this mecca, and kneeling by the graves of brave men, let the living clasp hands in fervency of friendship and strew sweet flowers upon the mouldering remains of our loyal dead.

A few more days and years will end our earthly career, but when we look, for the last time, upon that grand old flag, with its celestial colors, we will have the soul-lit satisfaction that our labor and blood, and that of our dear dead comrades, sustained it on the field of slaughter and transmitted it to posterity without a stripe extinguished or a star lost from its brilliant folds.

OLD SOLDIERS.

[Dedicated to George U. Morris Post, G. A. R., Georgetown, D. C.]

Our ranks are growing thinner, every year,
And Death is still a winner, every year;
   Yet, we still must stick together,
   Like the toughest kind of leather,
And in any kind of weather, every year.

Our comrades have departed, every year,
They leave us broken hearted, every year;
   But their spirits fondly greet us
   And they constantly entreat us
To come, that they may meet us, every year.

Our steps are growing slower, every year,
Pale Death is still a mower, every year;
   Yet, we faced him in the battle
   Amid the musket's rattle,
And defied his final edict, every year.

We are growing old and lonely, every year;
We have recollection only, every year;
   And we bled for this grand Nation
   On many a field and station
And with any kind of ration, every year.

Many people may forget us, every year,
And our enemies may fret us, every year;
   But, while onward we are drifting,
   Our souls with hope are lifting
To heavenly scenes still shifting, every year.

In the May-time of the flowers, every year,
We shall live in golden hours, every year;
   And our deeds be sung in story,
   Down the ages growing hoary
With a blaze of living glory, every year!

Leonadas, at Thermopalea; Horatio, at the bridge, and Wincklereid, at the ice-bound Swiss pass, were not inspired by more lofty courage than Grant in the Wilderness, Sheridan at Winchester, and Sherman in his March to the Sea.

The sunlight of liberty shone on their brow, and the love of home and country centered in their hearts. Monumental marble, granite, and bronze will long perpetuate their glorious deeds, but their name and fame at last rest in the hearts of the people and shall linger as long as suns and stars sparkle in their trackless spheres.

A thousand years my own Columbia shall be thy portion, until one grand universal Republic shall bless the world and its mammouth pillars rest on the broken bones of monarchy.

The self-styled lords of royalty must dismount from the backs of the people and work and walk in the ranks of mankind or depart forever from the surface of the globe.

The electric lights of science has lit up the rotten nooks of imperial dinasties and taught the people of all lands that those who pretend to rule by Divine right are but the leperous remains of robber barons and licentious queens.

The shining dome of our National Capitol, speaking through the lips of the Goddess of Liberty, calls to the down-trodden of foreign lands to fall into line and march westward, where the star of empire takes its course, and where the American Continent, with all its outlying islands, shall acknowledge no master but the American Congress and no flag but the Stars and Stripes!

> Not in vain the distance beckons;
> Forward, forward, let us range—
> Let the great world spin forever
> Down the ringing grooves of change.

We must build up the strongest navy that the world has ever known and erect coast defences that will resist all the forces that monarchy can send against us, and above all we must ingraft on our system of public schools, as well as in our colleges and universities, a perfect military education, where companies of soldiers and sailors may be graduated each year with the training of West Point and Annapolis.

When this is done the grasping, robbing, and murdering propensity of monarchy will respect the Monroe doctrine in letter and spirit and let this Republic forever alone.

Who will care for these loved mounds when we are gone? Who will then strew roses and plant bright flowers? Other patriotic hands of brave men and fair women will take up the roll of duty, and even when all but liberty has perished from the earth, the robin and the blue bird, the jay and the mocking bird, will warble at sunrise a reveille over the green sod that wraps their sacred clay. Nature herself will deck the graves of our fallen comrades, and the winds of Heaven will chant a requiem to their memory, and kiss the loved spot where valor sleeps.

Thousands of our dear, loved comrades rest in unknown graves far away from the loved ones at home. They slumber in the land of strangers, where the tears of love cannot moisten the green shroud that mantles their ashes. But if no kind hand is there to strew flowers, or loved eye to shed the tear of sorrow, there is One that reigns among the eternal stars that daily floods the unknown grave with sunshine, and nightly waters the budding wild flowers with dews from Heaven.

> Let Summer send her golden sunbeams down—
> In graceful salutations for the dead,
> And Autumn's host of leaflets brown,
> "Break ranks," above the fallen soldier's head,
> And we survivors of the fearful strife,
> While gathered here around their sacred clay,
> Let us anew pledge honor, fortune, life,
> That from our flag no star shall pass away.
> We reverently swear by all we love,
> By all we are, and all we hope to be,
> Yon starry flag, man's steadfast friend shall prove
> And wave forever o'er the brave and free!

III.

EMANCIPATION DAY.

In August, 1873, I delivered the following oration before five thousand colored people at St. Louis on the occasion of their Emancipation celebration:

FELLOW CITIZENS: The emancipation of an enslaved race is a theme fit to be couched in noble eloquence, monumented in bronze, and sent to the latest posterity in poetry and song. From the earliest dawn of creation, when the morning stars sang together, human thoughts and human action lingered at the shrine of freedom; and even in the night of Egyptian darkness and bondage, the sweet pæns of liberty sounded in the soul of man and found a responsive echo in the celestial realms of the angels.

God, in his infinite wisdom, created all men free, and it was only tyrants who could forge the chains of slavery and find consolation in the sharp music of the lash. Ignorance, selfishness, and fear make a man a tyrant, while intelligence, benevolence, and love fit him for the priceless blessings of freedom in this world, and open a way to his eternal home beyond the sun and stars.

The celebration of this day will bring vividly to your mind the trials and tribulations and victories achieved by your race in the West India Islands, where the genius of Toussaint L'Ouverture held at bay the cruelties of the proud Spaniard, and even foiled the expections of the great Napoleon. The pen and voice of L'Ouverture exposed the flimsy pretense of slavery, and his flashing sword cut in twain the Gordian knot of despotism and initiated the first successful emancipation movement. Today, in the mountain cabins of Hayti and San Domingo, the name of this apostle of liberty is sounded with love and veneration, and as the circling years go by, the fame of Toussaint L'Ouverture will grow brighter until every human heart pulsates with the sublime sentiments that actuated him in life, and made him a conqueror even in the torturing hours of death in the dungeon of the tyrant. The clanking chains of Napoleon and the excruciating pangs of cold, thirst, and hunger could not subdue the proud spirit of the black warrior and statesman. His free soul and glorious nature triumphed over the grave, and long after you and I are consigned to the dust from whence we sprung, this hero of San Domingo will live in monumental greatness, and inspire the world with his example.

L'Ouverture laid broad and deep the foundation of the Republic of San Domingo, and the day is near when the Stars and Stripes shall float over the land he died to save. God will work in his mysterious way, until the continent of Africa shall be disenthralled from the darkness of ignorance and slavery, when one universal Republic shall bless the world and realize the fondest hopes of the human heart. The wail of oppressed humanity comes sounding down the centuries; the cry for liberty and light is wafted to us in every breeze that blows from ocean's boundless shores.

> "Hark! our brothers call,
> From Greenland's icy mountains,
> From India's coral strand;
> Where Afric's sunny fountains
> Roll down their golden sand.
> From many an ancient river;
> From many a palmy plain;
> They call us to deliver
> Their land from error's chain."

In the year 1620, two hundred and fifty-three years ago, *forty-five* slaves were landed on the James River in Virginia, forced from the coast of Africa and sold into bondage to cultivate the plantations of the Old Dominion. From this "direful spring" Columbia has suffered more unnumbered woes than Achilles' wrath brought to Greece. I can see now in the jungles of Africa the fierce spirit of Caucasian cupidity hunting down the first load of human freight. The simple life of the black man in his native wilds knew no master but his God, pictured in the rising sun, and smiling in the blue waters of the Nile and Ganges.

I see that fatal ship stealing quietly out from the golden sands of Africa, speeding on its way to America, freighted with human misery and terrible grief. Would to God that she had sunk to the bottom of the ocean, and buried forever, even the just and the unjust, ere her prow touched the shores of Virginia, and began that reign of slavery that cursed our country and culminated in the great conflict of 1861.

Great crimes deserve great punishment, and fearful has been our retribution. Two millions of human lives were sacrificed to purchase the emancipation of American slavery, and today the tears of the widows and orphans flow at the mention of those loved hearts that went down into the dark valley of death in the musical whiz of the Minie rifle, or the roar of the Rodman gun.

The colored people of this Nation have great cause to boast of the deeds of their heroes. The first blood shed in the American Revolution was that of Crispus Attucks, of Boston, Mass. In the Massacre of March 5, 1770, in an assault upon the British soldiers he fell for freedom and his native land. The blood of the slave has nourished the tree of liberty, and under its wide-spreading branches you sit today basking in the sunshine of equal rights, proud of your citizenship and ready at all times to strike for—

> "The land of the free
> And the home of the brave!"

The freedom of American slavery required long years of education and toil. Adams, Jefferson, Clay, Garrison, and Phillips dug from the mountains the crude ore of liberty, but it was left to Lincoln, Seward, and Grant to put it through the furnace-heat of the Rebellion and forge out the trip-hammer that knocked forever the rusty shackles from four millions of slaves. The emancipation proclamation of Abraham Lincoln broke the back of the Rebellion. Its thunder-tones will go sounding down the ages, and the lightning flash of each sentence will irradiate the rugged road of the human race and light up the darkest nooks of imperial government. The memory of Lincoln will live as long as human hearts pulsate with love of liberty.

Rooted firmly and deeply in the rifted rocks of time shall be his temple of everlasting glory. The mountains of Columbia lifting their heads into the boundless blue, and the murmuring rivers of the continent, shall mingle forever with his fame, but the noblest monument to his memory are the four million shackles struck from the galling limbs of the bondsmen. Already the lesson of the proclamation has found its way to the plains of the Amazon and the bleak regions of the Ural Mountains, where twenty million Russian serfs breathe at last the pure air of freedom. So shall the example of the immortal Lincoln continue to bless the human race, until, crowned with the diadem of liberty, we shall acknowledge the image of God in all men, and pluck from the calendar of our hearts the demon of caste and persecution.

From my earliest years I hated the very name of slavery. The word burned upon my tongue and blistered in my heart. Even as a boy, in the land of Clay, I sighed for the hour to strike at the hell-born iniquity; and when the clash of arms came I went out to battle for the perpetuation of the Union and the freedom of the slave. The first shot at Sumter sounded the death-knell of slavery, and it will echo in the hearts of generations yet unborn, until every land and clime hears the sweet songs of liberty, and joins in the chorus of equality.

Your own stout arms and valiant hearts struggled in the cause of freedom. Port Hudson and Fort Wagner will long be remembered as among the bloodiest battles of the war, where the First Louisiana and Fifty-fourth Massachusetts colored regiments fought with terrible desperation, and made a page in American history that will transmit the glory of the black warrior to the last symbol of recorded time.

Since the close of the war the behavior of the black man has been truly remarkable, for never in the history of the world did men come up so quick out of the dark forests of ignorance and bondage, and show such capacity for civil life and constitutional freedom. Lift up your eyes and hearts to God, and never despair. Seven centuries ago the Caucasian race was wandering half naked in the black forests of Germany, and the Scots and Picts of proud Albion were little above the wild animals that furnished their food and raiment.

In the Senate of the United States and Lower House of Congress, representatives of your race have sat side by side with white men, and have maintained their independence and manhood. Today you stand upon the same political platform with the greatest and best of your white fellow citizens, and even those who once held you in bondage have become reconciled to the logic of events. Forget, if you can, the cruelties of slavery in the gratitude you owe the Nation for clothing you with the inestimable power of the ballot—

> " A weapon that comes down as still
> As snow-flakes falling on the sod,
> And executes a freeman's will
> As lightning does the will of God!"

In conclusion, let me impress upon you the great importance of temperance, economy, education, and peaceful conduct toward your neighbors. Whether as laborers, mechanics, merchants, or professionals, you must rely upon yourselves, and by untiring perseverance and honesty procure a home, where the blessings of peace and prosperity shall crown the evening of life, and give you a taste of that immortal happiness found only in the beautiful land around the white throne of Jehovah, where the angels always sing and the light of Heaven shines eternal.

IV.

A TOAST TO WOMAN.

[At a Brooklyn St. Patrick's Banquet.]

Woman is a great subject. I cannot imagine why you should always leave her until one of the last of the list of toasts, unless it be that when all else has departed man naturally flies to woman for consolation. The most endearing words are sweetheart, sister, daughter, wife, mother, and the keystone to this royal arch of purity and love is woman. The touch of her warm hand lulls the sleeping babe to sweet repose, the glance of her beaming eye thrills the soul of manhood, and in the golden sunlight of old age she clings with undying affection to the object of her love. Pure and patient at the cradle, faithful and enduring at the cross, she will receive the crown of immortal life beyond the sun and stars. In every land and clime the advancement of woman points to the pathway of civilization, and, although she speaks in various tongues, her language of love is universal, and her influence in home, church, and State marks the mile-stones of human progress. History is full of heroic women who led armies, died for the liberty of their country, and suffered the tortures of battle and the pangs of hospital experience. Cleopatra, the lovely Egyptian queen, the Maid of Orleans, whose white banner proclaimed victory; Charlotte Corday, the peasant girl, who killed a heartless tyrant, and Florence Nightingale, the charity angel of modern times, are niched in historic grandeur, and ages yet unborn will sing the glory of their proud renown. But while these heroines of history have left the impress of their genius upon the world, the quiet, loving, patient, heroine of home, who toils for the child and man she loves, claims most my respect and admiration. In the silent watches of the night she stoops with a nervous, listening ear over the pale face of the dying boy, and in her breaking heart holds his image to the grave. The bed of pain, the gloomy prison, the gallows, and the grave find her ministering hand, and she is always ready to throw the mantle of charity over a fallen mortal and soothe the anguish of misfortune in the deepest vale of adversity.

Who has not heard of the sad fate of the talented and beautiful Miss Curran, the affianced bride of Robert Emmet, a young hero who lived for Ireland and her friends, and died for the immortal principles of right. The green graves of the broken-hearted beauty and her noble lover are the brightest gems in the crown of Ireland's sorrow, and in the coming years they will shine as diadems in her crown of victory.

> "Pile thick the amaranth and the myrtle o'er them,
>   Let bright, green banners flash and flow,
> Roses that love and pansies that deplore them,
>   And lilies weeping from their hearts of snow!"

I shall never forget a scene during the late war. At the battle of Kennesaw Mountain, near Atlanta, I was wounded and left on the field to die. After a terrible encounter between the contending armies of Sherman and Johnson, the sun went down upon that fraternal slaughter.

> Our bugles sang trace while the night clouds had lowered,
>   And the sentinel stars set their watch in the sky,
> And thousands had sunk on the ground overpowered,
>   The weary to sleep and the wounded to die.

In that terrible moment, left in the woods to the night winds and the twinkling stars, dying with pain and thirst, I beheld two angelic forms move over the battlefield, and as they approached my prostrate form, with kind words and water to quench my burning thirst, I recognized two Sisters of Charity, whose white hoods shown like celestial light brought down from Heaven to cheer the drooping heart of man. Such is woman, fondest in decay, greatest in adversity, and best in everything.

> Here's a toast, then to woman, heart true and free.
> Who quaffs off a cup to memory and me,
> And wafts o'er the billows sighs of regret
> For hours that are gone and suns that are set,
> And changeless as fate, who loves to the close
> Her wandering hero through strife and repose,
> Fresh in her beauty as dew on the rose.

POETIC PEBBLES.

THE STORY OF THE SAGE.

[Dedicated to Goldwin Patten, actor.]

I met a sage, decrepit, old, and gray,
While plodding through his last declining day,
And asked him, as he wandered down the vale,
To tell me of his life's eventful tale.
He leant upon his staff and paused awhile,
Then gazed across the sea to some fair isle
That met his fading vision through the gloom,
Where roses blossom in eternal bloom.
Fair youth, he said, my well-remembered years
Arise before me now through smiles and tears,
And take me back to love-lit, golden hours,
When life was young, amid sweet fragrant flowers;
My hopes were of the golden time to be,
Or like a full-rigged ship upon the sea—
Freighted with all the flashing hues of mind
That thrill the soul or deify mankind.
My boyhood pleasure was as bright as thine—
Came lightly as the foam on rosy wine;
But like the foam it quickly passed away
And left me to another doubtful day.
I fondly thought that when my manhood came
I'd rush into the ranks and win a name
That ages yet unborn would emulate,
And grant me glory in both Church and State.
In blooming age I sought for power and place,
And won distinction in full many a race;
But just as sweet perfection came to view
The bowl was dashed and left me trials anew.

I sought the field of glory and of war,
My hope as bright as yonder evening star;
And there I heard the shot and shrieking shell
That roared in terror, like a voice from hell.
Upon the ramparts high I waved my flag,
And struggled bravely up the mountain crag;
But just as victory o'er me threw her spell
I dropped the flag, faltered, wounded fell.
A broken soldier who has known defeat
Can fight and fall, but never can retreat,
And now you see me just the sport of Fate,
Its taunting voice still ringing out—too late.
In legislative halls with words ornate
I shone amid the thunders of debate,
And reaped some glory with a loud applause
For making many wholesome, honest laws.
I walked among the noble and the great
Who stood as pillars to the rising State;
And while Dame Fortune promised every prize,
I only caught a glimpse of her bright eyes.
Yes, I have known a loving maid's embrace,
Whose soul shone brightly in her cheering face,
While laughing children clambered on my knee,
And blessed me with the glory of their glee.
Yet these have gone and left me weak and lone,
With nothing here that I can call my own,
Like yon bare pine that topples to decay,
And droops above where all its fellows lay;
Or like an eagle on some mountain height,
With longing eyes, peers through the gathering night,
Awaiting one that never shall again
Soar with him grandly o'er the hill and plain.
Then I had friends who filled my banquet hall,
They drank my sparkling wine, both one and all;
But when they saw and knew that I might fall,
They left me rudely with life's bitter gall!
But why repine for pleasure that is past,
Or sigh for earthly power that cannot last;
While people praise us for their fame and joy
Erecting idols they will soon destroy?
I wandered many years in foreign lands

From arctic regions to bright tropic sands,
Seeking for perfect pleasure on the way,
But never found it to the present day.
In beauty's eyes, from Persia to Peru,
I caught love glances as they darted through
The veil that cruel custom seeks to hide
What nature gave to show with honest pride.
In Florence and in Rome I looked aghast
At works of art that told me of the past,
Which peopled every crumbling tower and pile
With royal spirits from some fairy isle.
The glowing canvas and the marble bust
Have rescued heroes from the thickening dust
That centuries of time accumulate
Upon the name of those who serve the State;
But yet, the time will come when even the great
Are lost within the ruins of their State,
And every glorious fame that thrilled the past
Shall perish from the earth and die at last.
Ah! here today you find me old and gray,
A wreck where once ambition held its sway;
Where every romance in the soul of youth
Came lightly as the angel of the truth.
Now you are young, and like the noble pine,
But sure as fate, your steps must follow mine—
While you may hear and see what I have seen,
Your name be mentioned in immortal green;
Yet still remember that no power or gold
Can purchase an exemption to grow old.
One hundred years have crowned my troubled way,
And here I crumble with my mother clay;
I'll take a last long look at yonder sun:
Farewell! farewell! My fleeting life is done!
He ceased, and sank into the gloom of night,
And left behind no ray of cheering light,
While all his conversation did but seem
The vestige of a vain and vanished dream!

DECORATION DAY POEM.

[Oak Hill Cemetery, May 30, 1895.]

Grand Home of the Dead! we mourn as we tread
   Near the forms that crumble below;
How sad and how still the graves on Oak Hill,
   'Neath the sunlight in bright golden glow.

Here's a rough, rude stone, moss-grown and alone,
   Where old Time has left not a trace
Of the name it bore in the days of yore,
   After brain and body ceased race.

Vain, vain is the thought; no one ever bought
   Exemption from final decay—
To live and to rot, and then be forgot,
   The fate of the quick of today.

The soldier and sage from age unto age
   Have slept 'neath these towering trees;
The young and the old, the bright and the bold
   Are sung by the breath of the breeze.

Brave Babcock in peace here finds his surcease
   From sorrows that troubled his life;
And rests with his God, beneath the green sod,
   Away from this cold world of strife.

Here Reno retires from war's flaming fires
   To shine with immortals above,
And bivouac there, devoid of all care,
   In realms of infinite love.

Here Morris, the brave, a king of the wave,
   Doth slumber beneath the old flag;
Hero so grand, on the famed "Cumberland,"
   And bold as a tall mountain crag.

While ocean shall roar on rock-beaten shore
   The memory of Morris shall be
A great loyal light for freedom's fair fight
   On river, on land, and on sea.

And Stanton; the grand, stood out for this land,
　　When Rebellion reared up its fierce face;
Calmly reposes 'neath beds of sweet roses—
　　A lone hero, in war's ruin race.

His great iron arm kept the Union from harm
　　While he smashed all the foes in its way—
As great Lincoln, his Chief, looked on with deep grief
　　At the war 'twixt the Blue and the Gray.

As years roll along, with sorrow or song,
　　His name shall grow braver and brighter—
A Puritan true, who knew what to do
　　With soldiers and Grant, the great fighter.

Here sleeps fine Van Ness who knew no distress,
　　While Burns expended his gold,
A Senator true, who b'lieved in the Blue,
　　A gentleman honest and bold.

Great Lorenzo Dow, who never knew how
　　To garnish his truth with a lie,
Sleeps under these flowers through May's golden hours,
　　Illumined by the sun and the sky.

Here, Corcoran, the sage, Bishop Pinckney, broad gauge,
　　Repose under marble so white;
They've gone to a land, bright, blooming, and grand,
　　Where never, up there, is a night.

Here, John Howard Payne sings again that refrain
　　That thrills us wherever we roam;
O'er land or o'er sea, our hearts still shall be
　　The Mecca of dear Home, Sweet Home.

O'er the flight of the years, with smiles or with tears,
　　The memory of Payne shall remain;
And millions unborn, in twilight and morn
　　Shall sing his immortal refrain.

Let soldier and sage from age unto age
　　Richly have all their merit and praise;
But the poet will be a light for the free
　　To the end of our last, dawning days.

Count Bodisco sleeps here, where trees shed a tear
   O'er the grave of the Muscovite peer—
Away from all ill he rests on Oak Hill,
   A memory from year unto year.

Dick Merrick lies here, a bright, brilliant seer.
   A lawyer of lingering renown,
Who fought every wrong of the cruel and strong
   In county or city or town.

Here rests the bright Blaine, in sunshine and rain,
   Who left his imprint on the Nation,
A keen, brainy mind, devoted and kind,
   Well fitted to fill a great station.

No shaft marks his grave to tell traveler or slave
   Where that proud, loyal heart lowly lies;
Yet the tall pines of Maine sigh in sorrow for Blaine
   As they toss their green heads to the skies.

Our sweet little child, so simple and mild,
   Sleeps here under roses so fair;
Yet, soon we shall go to a clime where no woe
   Or sighs can corrode us with care.

Mother and sister, sweetheart and wife,
   Repose from their labors on earth;
Resting alone, away from all strife,
   Where the soul finds a happy, new birth.

Yet the citizens dead have always been wed
   To Liberty, Friendship, and Truth—
Must be honored as well as soldiers who fell
   In the pride of their brave, loyal youth.

Then, strew sweetest flowers o'er the soldier,
   But remember the citizen, too,
Who stood by his conscience in trouble—
   And supported the Gray or the Blue.

God bless our grand Nation forever,
   God bless every heart, fond and true;
God bless any soul that won't sever,
   The Gray from the Red, White, and Blue!

GRANT'S MUSTERED OUT!

Half-mast the flag, a heart brave and stout
Surrenders at last; Grant's mustered out;
Toll the bell slowly, moisten his sod,
Peace to his ashes, glory to God!

Battle and trial shall never again
Harrow the hero in sunshine or rain;
Gone to a land devoid of all doubt;
His service is over—Grant's mustered out.

His fame, like a light; shall shine through the years,
Hallowed by memory and watered by tears—
Flags that he carried shall long flap and flout,
A record of glory is not mustered out!

Donelson, Shiloh, the Wilderness too,
Milestones immortal with deeds of the Blue:
And this is the man that never knew rout,
Till Fate told the world that—Grant's mustered out.

Nations unborn shall visit his tomb,
Reared by the people, and lasting as doom,—
Mecca where manhood may kneel without doubt,
Truth everlasting is not mustered out!

KATIE AND I.

[Suggested by my wife.]

Katie and I sat singing, singing
  As the moon went down;
While bells were loudly ringing, ringing
  In the far-off town.

Katie and I sat thinking, thinking
  Of the long ago;
Sweet baby fingers lightly linking
  Memories under snow.

Katie and I soon sleeping, sleeping
  'Neath the silent sod;
Our spirits fondly greeting, greeting
  Children, rest and God.

FAREWELL.

Farewell! farewell! My heart is sad and lonely,
   While sailing o'er life's surging, stormy sea;
My soul-lit thoughts are centered in thee only—
   The sweetest being in my memory.

Farewell! farewell! The secret of my longing
   Cannot be told to those of common clay—
Yet, from the past your plighted vows come thronging,
   And thrill me with a love that could not stay.

Farewell! farewell! My bark is on the billow
   That hastens onward to a foreign shore;
I fain would rest upon a fevered pillow,
   And still my weary soul forevermore.

Farewell! farewell! Another hand shall lead thee,
   Another heart has won the prize I sought;
Why, Oh! why could you rebuke, deceive me,
   And leave me lonely with this killing thought?

Farewell! farewell! Thus are we doomed to sever,
   And break the tie that bound us to the past;
Yet in my heart, forever and forever,
   I'll keep your sainted image to the last.

BY THE SEA.

I am standing by the sea,
   And I listen to the roar
Of the mighty ocean,
   As it breaks against the shore.

I think of Now and Then,
   And long for evermore
To taste of living wine
   On God's eternal shore.

I see the breaker coming,
   With a petrel on its crest;
I plunge into the billow,
   Wildly crying, "Here is rest!"

TOLL THE BELL.

Toll the bell slowly, meekly, and lowly,
  There comes an inanimate clod,
Sleeping forever beyond the dark river
  A mortal has gone to his God.

Toll the bell faintly; echoes so saintly
  Are sounding o'er river and lea,
Telling the living all need forgiving
  Before God and eternity.

Toll the bell lightly, daily and nightly
  A spirit is watching for thee,
One that has loved us, one that has proved us,
  Some fond soul who loved you and me.

Toll the bell sadly, heart-broken, madly
  We kiss the cold lips of the dead,
With hope, love, and tears, run back o'er the years
  To pluck out some cruel word said.

FLOWERS OF HOPE.

[Dedicated to M. J. Murphy.]

The sweetest flowers of golden hours
  Must fade and pass away;
But love or truth, of age or youth,
  Shall never know decay.

The hills are gray. Old Time won't stay,
  But keeps upon the wing;
Its flight of years bring smiles and tears
  To peasant, prince, and king.

Dear friends, depart; and leave the heart—
  A ruin old and lone—
With nothing here, from year to year,
  Which it can call its own.

Yet, o'er the gloom beyond the tomb,
  Where Hope can only see,
There is a rest among the blessed,
  And joy for you and me.

FORGETTING.

The friends that I loved in December
    And cherished so fondly in May,
Have long since forgot to remember,
    And vanished like dewdrops away.

In sunshine and power I was toasted
    And feasted by courtiers so kind;
And, Oh! how the parasites boasted
    Of the wonderful traits of my mind.

But when the dark hour of my trouble
    Arose like a storm in the sky,
The vipers began to play double,
    And forgot the bright glance of my eye!

THE IRISHMAN.

[Dedicated to Pat Hoban.]

As orator, poet, and soldier
    He stands in the front of the line;
No mortal was ever more bolder
    To live on the classical wine.

His heart is as big as the mountains,
    His soul sighs for beauty and grace;
His mind drinks at all of the fountains
    Where knowledge and love run apace.

His wit, like the dews of the morning,
    Enlivens the weight of an hour;
His proud heart has nothing but scorning
    For tyrants who pivot on power.

For freedom he'll fight on forever,
    And never surrender to wrong;
His love for the truth you can't sever;
    His home is a sigh and a song.

Then hurrah for old Erin, the Emerald,
    That shines as the gem of the sea,
And her brave sons who never surrender
    To vultures of king's tyranny.

THE SUNBEAM.

A beautiful beam came into my cell,
Fresh from the eye of Jehovah, to tell
That bolts and bars cannot keep out the light
Of truth, and justice, of mercy and right;
It checkered the flags through the iron door,
And danced in the shadows that kissed the floor,
And loitered about in a friendly way,
Until beckoned back at the close of day;
When out of the window, it flew on high
And hastened back to its home in the sky.
I followed the beautiful beam to rest,
To a sea of light in the golden west;
It dropped to sleep on the dark blue sea
And left me the sweetest memory.
I turned to my soul for calm relief,
Balm to my wound, a check to my grief—
When visions of glory shone from above
Where the light is God, and God is love!

MY BABY'S EYES.

[To Florence.]

My baby's eyes in melting blue
Are beaming bright as morning dew,
And from the skylight take a hue,
Or like the starlight bright and true.

My baby's eyes in liquid roll
Enhance my world from pole to pole,
And love sits smiling in that goal
Forever speaking to my soul.

My baby's eyes in other years
May fill with many scalding tears,
And yet through cruel taunts and jeers
A mother's love will banish fears.

My baby's eyes in blight or bloom,
Those glorious orbs in grief or gloom,
Shall be to me in death or doom,
The dearest diamonds to the tomb.

THE LEAVES ARE FALLING.

[Dedicated to my daughter, Libbie.]

The leaves are falling; I hear you calling
  From out the years that slumber in the past,
Asleep or waking, my heart is breaking
  For one sweet love that thrills it to the last.

The leaves are sailing, and I'm bewailing
  The lost affections of my vanished youth,
When friends were nearer, and hearts were dearer,
  And life was in the heaven of their truth.

The leaves are flying, the winds are sighing,
  And Nature in her garb of green and gray
Makes many changes o'er hills and ranges—
  A bride of beauty in her autumn day.

Along the hours, in golden showers
  The leaves are falling over hill and dale;
Their ranks are broken—a voiceless token
  That we shall follow down the fading vale
  And perish like the leaves blown by the gale!

GOD IS NEAR.

[Dedicated to Rev. David Wills, of Georgia.]

God is near upon the ocean,
  God is near upon the land;
He is All, both rest and motion—
  We are only grains of sand.
Little mites upon life's billow,
  May-flies buzzing out the hour,
Dreams upon a fevered pillow—
  Dewdrops on a withered flower;
Only waiting for tomorrow—
  That has never come to man,
Here we live in joy and sorrow,
  Chasing phantoms as we can,
Chasing pleasure, chasing greatness,
  Over tangled walks and waves;
But we learn the bitter lateness

Just before we find our graves.
Hope is nigh with fairy fingers,
   Tracing sunbeams on the way;
Magic memory ever lingers,
   Busy with the bygone day.
Life and death are but the portals
   To a realm of endless rest;
God is working through his mortals;
   All in some way shall be blessed!

THE EXILE.

In other lands beyond the sea,
My thoughts will often turn to thee;
And gazing o'er the billows' crest
My heart shall travel to the West,
Where lies a home, the sweetest, best.

Fair land of pine and oak and ash,
Where sparkling streams forever dash,
Mid mountain crags so grand and old
Rock-ribbed with iron, silver, gold,
And fertile fields of generous mould.

The friends I knew in childhood years
Are seen with love through smiles and tears
And as my bounding bark departs—
One look, one sigh, to tender hearts—
How memory from my bosom starts!

How oft my eyes will turn in vain
To see my native land again,
And as the sail departs from view,
I'll peer across the ocean blue
To catch one glimpse of love and yon.

But I am destined still to roam,
Without a country or a home,
A lonely exile bent with care.
A barren waste, both bleak and bare—
No friend to cheer me anywhere.

THE OLD HOMESTEAD.

[Dedicated to Hon. Amos Cummings, New York.]

I gaze on my old ruined homestead today
    Through the tears of a wild, vanished youth;
I see the broad porches gone down to decay
    Where my mother instilled every truth.

The chimney has crumbled away in the blast,
    And the rafters have all tumbled down;
The hearthstone brings back all the joys of the past
    As the clouds in the west darkly frown.

The spring at the foot of the hill has gone dry,
    And the apple and plum trees have gone;
I stand in the gloom as the winds deeply sigh—
    See the ghosts of my friends one by one.

Here, my mother and father sleep side by side
    In a nook on the top of the hill;
Where my heart was as light as the foam on the tide
    When I sauntered about the old mill.

That stood on the banks of the creek, down the lane,
    Where it rumbled its musical flow;
But alas! I shall never play there again
    As I played in the sweet long ago.

The woodpecker drums o'er my head on the oak
    And the gray squirrel chatters his tune,
But where are the schoolmates whose sport and whose joke
    Thrilled my heart in the play-spell at noon.

Some are "gone o'er the ranges" to sleep in the vale;
    Like myself, some have wandered afar—
Blown about like a leaf in a withering gale
    Or attuned like a broken guitar!

By the last ray of sunset I sadly behold
    The old ruined home of my youth,
Where the jessamine clambered in colors of gold,
    And the voices I heard spoke the truth.

Farewell to the scenes and the friends that I knew
    In the morning of life, bright and fair—
My heart shall forever commingle with you
    And my spirit shall always be there!

THERE'S NO POCKET IN A SHROUD!

[On the death of a millionaire.]

You must leave your many millions
  And the gay and festive crowd;
Though you roll in royal billions,
  There's no pocket in a shroud.

Whether pauper, prince, or peasant;
  Whether rich or poor or proud—
Remember that there isn't
  Any pocket in a shroud.

You'll have all this world of glory
  With a record long and loud,
And a name in song and story,
  But no pocket in your shroud.

So be gen'rous with your riches,
  Neither vain, nor cold, nor proud,
And you'll gain the golden niches
  In a clime without a cloud!

I WALK ALONE.

[Dedicated to Walt Whitman.]

I walk alone where morning beams are shining,
  And winds are blowing o'er the stormy sea;
I look aloft and see a silver lining
  That thrills my soul with thoughts of Deity.

I walk alone where evening shadows lower,
  Peering through the crimson clouds of fate;
My heart beats out the lagging, weary hour,
  Repeating to my soul—too late, too late.

I walk alone where mountain streams are leaping,
  And snow-capped summits reach unto the sky,
And still my nightly, silent watch I'm keeping,
  Gazing into worlds beyond that never die.

I walk alone the rugged road of life,
  Where human "may-flies" flutter, fly, and fall;
I battle still with everlasting strife—
  Ambition, glory, and the grave—that's all!

UNKNOWN.

[Dedicated to Mack Lipscomb, Washington, D. C.]

I gazed on the babe at its mother's breast,
And asked for the secret of life and rest;
It turned with a smile that was sad and lone,
And murmured in dreaming, "Unknown," "unknown."

I challenged the youth so bold and so brave,
To tell me the tale of the lonely grave;
But he sung of pleasure in musical tone,
And his echoing voice replied "Unknown," "unknown."

Then I questioned the gray-haired man of years,
Whose face was furrowed with thoughts and tears;
And he paused in his race to simply groan,
The soul-chilling words: "Unknown" "unknown."

I asked the lover, the poet, and sage—
In every clime and in every age—
To tell me the truth, and candidly own
If after life it is all unknown.

I soared like the lark to the boundless sky,
Sighed in my soul for the how and the why;
The angels were singing and just had flown;
I heard but the echo, "Unknown, "unknown."

I read in the hills and saw in the rocks
A lesson that told of the earthquake shocks;
I gazed at the stars from a mountain cone,
But they only answered—"Unknown," "unknown."

Thus am I tortured by fear and by doubts,
In tracing the way where so many routes
Are ever in view, and quickly are flown,
And all that I know is—"Unknown," "unknown."

At last I determined to surely find
All hope and all bliss in my mystic mind;
But just as sweet peace came to soothe me alone,
The wild witch of doubt shrieked: "Unknown," "unknown."

The sun and the moon, the winds and the wave,
May perish in time and sink to the grave;
The temples of earth shall fall, stone by stone,
And mortals still wail out—"Unknown," "unknown."

The millions of earth that battle today
Are but a handful to those passed away;
The future is countless—men from each zone
Shall flourish and die in the far-off unknown.

We come like the dewdrops and go like the mist,
As frail as a leaf by autumn winds kissed;
Fading away like the roses of June—
Wishing and waiting to meet the unknown.

Nature, Oh! Nature, thy God I adore;
There's light in thy realm, I ask for no more;
From the seed to the fruit all things are grown,
Yet, while we know this, the cause is unknown.

When matter and mind are perished and lost,
And all that we see into chaos is tossed,
From nothing to nothing we pass out alone,
Like a flash or an echo—"Unknown," "unknown."

WHEN I AM DEAD.

When I am dead let no vain pomp display,
A surface sorrow o'er my pulseless clay,
But all the dear old friends I loved in life
Can shed a tear, console my child and wife.

When I am dead let strangers pass me by,
Nor ask a reason for the how or why
That brought my wandering life to praise or shame,
Or marked me for the fading flowers of fame.

When I am dead, the vile assassin tongue
Will try and banish all the lies it flung,
And make amends for all its cruel wrong
In fulsome praise and eulogistic song.

When I am dead, what matters to the crowd?
The world will rattle on as long and loud,
And each one in the game of life will plod
The field to glory and the way to God.

When I am dead, some sage for self-renown
May urn my ashes in his native town,
And give, when I am cold, and lost, and dead,
A marble slab, where once I needed bread.

A FRIEND.

A friend is one who knows your fault,
   And knowing dares to chide you;
Who blisters wrong with Attic salt
   And still sticks close beside you.

A friend is one who lifts you up
   When sin and sorrow hover,
And casts aside the bitter cup
   And takes you under cover.

A frend is one whose words are true,
   Whose purse in trial or trouble
Is ever open unto you;
   Whose heart cannot play double.

A friend is one who bends alone
   Above your nameless tomb,
And keeps your memory all her own
   As flowers in full bloom.

A FIRESIDE MEMORY.

[Dedicated to Dominick I. Murphy, Washington, D. C.]

She's gone, yet memory unconfined
   Has reared a temple in my heart,
Where all her virtues are enshrined,
   That never from my soul depart.

Her voice, like music low and sweet,
   Could soothe me in the deepest woe—
How willing were her flying feet
   To serve me in the long ago.

Her face, like yonder bank of flowers,
   Shone brightly o'er me, near and far—
Lit up my life in lonely hours—
   My truest friend, my polar star.

No more those footsteps run to greet
   My lagging moments, night or day;
We never more on earth shall meet—
   My joys with her have passed away.

Her image hangs on yonder wall
   Still speaking of the olden time,
When she to me was all in all
   And love was in its early prime.

Now bending o'er the smouldering fire,
   I see the shadows come and go,
While one by one the sparks expire,
   And flake by flake comes down the snow.

But through the gloom I always see
   A ray of that dear vanished light,
And memory fondly brings to me
   Her image ever pure and bright.

AMONG THE HILLS.

Among the hills where summer rills
   Come leaping o'er the grasses,
I hear the glee from tree to tree
   And see the lads and lasses.

The laughing noise of girls and boys
   Awaken youthful dreaming
Of long ago, with joy and woe,
   And many bright eyes beaming.

But now today my hair is gray,
   The wrinkles o'er me creeping;
My youth is past, and here at last
   I'm left to silent weeping.

But memory clings and love still sings
   Among the hills of childhood,
The tunes I knew when friends were true,
   And pleasure ruled the wildwood.

Laugh on sweet youth, with love and truth
   Be happy without measure,
While song and rhyme can kill old Time
   And youth remains a treasure.

THE SUTLER.

"I will a Sutler be that profits may accrue.—SHAKSPEARE.

[Dedicated to the Grand Army of the Republic.]

I sing the song of the sutler,
  Who fought in the battle of life,
The song of the prize-package "artist,"
  Who never got into the strife;
Not the jubilant song of the soldier,
  Who never forgot to lay claim
To the greenbacks that stuck in the "Jack Pot"
  At the end of a winter-night game.
But the song of the beautiful sutler,
  Who traveled in sunshine and rain,
For the sake of the almighty dollar
  And whatever else he could gain;
And his youth bore no flower on its branches,
  But his age was a bright, sunny day;
For the prize that he gloriously grasped at
  Was the cash that he carried away.
And the work that he did for the Army
  In the rear of the soldiers was seen,
Where he set up his crackers and herrings,
  And the smell of the festive sardine
That he sold to the "boys" on a credit,
  Or the clamp of a paymaster's lease;
And six boxes he gave for five dollars,
  While the rest brought a dollar a piece.
While the world at large sheds a tear
  To the hero that may be bereft,
I drink to the Grand Army Sutler
  Who never was known to get left!
Who rushed to the front, when the camp-fires
  Lit up all the hills, without fear;
But at the first crack of the rifle
  He galloped away to the rear,
With his pipes, his tobacco, and whiskey,
  And his barrels of sour lager beer;
And he never let up on his running
  Till the Long Bridge appeared to his view,

Where he opened up shop in his wagon,
    And roped-in the gay " boys in blue."
How he held to his faith unseduced,
    With the glint of the cash in his eye;
And for this great cause how he suffered!
    For the cash, not the country, he'd die!
Then rear to the sutler a temple,
    Of granite and brass that will stay,
Where the spirit of Shylock shall hover,
    And beam on the "blue" and the "gray,"
Who once paid a tribute to genius,
    With a gall that no mortal could rule,
And a smile like a lightning-rod peddler,
    And a cheek like the Grand Army Mule!

MY NATIVE LAND.

[Dedicated to the memory of my father.]

Farewell to the land of my birth and my childhood,
    Where the shamrock and hawthorn bloom in the vale,
And the linnet and thrush sing sweet in the wildwood;
    Where perfume of roses is borne on the gale.

Farewell to the hills and the streams where I wandered,
    To my dear mountain cot at the edge of the glen,
Where often, in spring-time, I played and I pondered,
    But ne'er shall I witness those loved scenes again.

Farewell to the church and the school-house of learning,
    To the lads and the lasses that frolicked in glee;
My heart is near breaking while footsteps are turning
    To a land full of freedom far over the sea.

Farewell to the grave of my father and mother;
    The daisy and violet bloom o'er their head;
The turf is still fresh on the breast of another—
    The dearest and sweetest of those with the dead.

Farewell, we must part, and the links of love sever,
    Yet tears of remembrance for thee shall renew
The friendship I'll cherish forever and ever
    Wherever I wander, dear Erin, for you!

THE SHAMROCK.

(Dedicated to Dr. P. S. O'Reilley, St. Louis, Mo.)

There's a green little plant that grows over the sea,
    That I love, although far, far away,
And its petals are always the dearest to me,
    For they bloom in my heart night and day.

The rose and the lily are fine to behold,
    With the perfume distilled from their cells,
But more precious to me than diamonds or gold
    Is the tale that the green shamrock tells.

It tells of a faith that has never been crushed,
    And a people you cannot subdue,
Of echoes of freedom that never are hushed—
    Like the roar of the ocean we view.

It whispers a song of sweet dreams that are fled,
    Of bright hopes that have vanished away—
Of heroes of freedom who fought and who bled,
    Of bards with their musical lay.

Though the harp of the bard may be broken,
    And the voice of the singer be still,
The green shamrock is ever our token—
    For it blooms over valley and hill.

Where the thrush and the blackbird and linnet
    Sing their notes to the rivers that run,
And the lark can be seen every minute,
    As he circles around to the sun.

LET ME REST.

Let me rest where sunlight lingers,
    'Neath the waving willow shade,
Where the morn with dewy fingers
    Sprinkles diamonds o'er the glade.

Where the little birds are singing
    O'er the flowers above my tomb,
And the matin bells are ringing
    Mortals to celestial bloom!

VANITY.

[Dedicated to Henry T. Stanton, Kentucky.]

Sweet thoughts that we cannot repeat,
    And songs that we never can sing
Arise in the brain but to meet
    And speed like a bird on the wing.

A light or a flash on the wave,
    Is the life that we live today—
A memory gone to the grave,
    Or the laugh of a child at play.

A glance at this world of beauty,
    A bubble that floats on the sea;
To hope and to die for duty,
    And sink to eternity.

KISSING O'ER THE BARS.

[A Song. Dedicated to "Gypsy Kroh."]

I had a little sweetheart, her name was Jennie Lee,
We met down by the brooklet, and by the waters free,
We clasped and kissed each other, beneath the rising stars—
Our hearts kept tune together while kissing o'er the bars.

Although the years have left me and I am old and gray,
I can't forget the gloaming that long since passed away;
Yet while my life is wasting and marked by many scars,
I'm standing by the brooklet and kissing o'er the bars!

Often in the evening when I gaze across the sea,
My soul is filled with rapture for home and Jennie Lee,
And though a lonely exile exposed to jolts and jars,
I'm kissing, fondly kissing, my sweet Jennie o'er the bars!

She left me in the morning when life was young and true;
Her spirit shines upon me from yonder bounding blue,
And though the world rebukes me with many winds and wars,
My heart and soul feel rapture while kissing o'er the bars!

THE THISTLE.

[Dedicated to Thomas Somerville, Sr., Washington, D. C.]

Let England boast of ivy green,
　Of beef and gold and gristle;
But still my soul shall always lean
　To Scotland and its thistle.

Old Ireland may its shamrock praise,
　Romantic airs still whistle;
Yet give me back my childhood days—
　Dear Scotland and its thistle.

Gay France may boast the lily white,
　Its slopes with vines may bristle,
Yet all its joys both day and night
　Can't vie with Scotland's thistle.

Columbia, my adopted land,
　Sweet liberty, thy story;
To thee I freely give my hand,
　My heart for Scotland's glory.

The land of Wallace, Bruce, and Burns,
　Refreshed by Highland misle,
To thee my throbbing heart still turns,
　My Scotland and its thistle.

'Tis there the bonny Doon and Ayr
　Reflect the evening shadow,
With thistles growing everywhere
　'Mid mountain, marsh, and meadow.

JUST SO.

Our vices are printed in "caps,"
　Our virtues in small "nonpareil;"
And all of our daily mishaps
　The neighbors are ready to tell.

If you stumble, beware of the crowd—
　It's callous, and heartless, and cold;
'Twill praise you today long and loud;
　Tomorrow, 'twill damn brave and bold!

THE VOICE OF THE CLOCK.

[Dedicated to Derwin De Forest, of New York.]

Tick, tick, the moments fly,
Tick, tick, we live and die.
Tick, tick, goes the hour,
Tick, tick, fades the flower.

Tick, tick, heartbeats go,
Tick, tick, weal or woe.
Tick, tick, soon are fled,
Tick, tick, lost and dead.

Tick, tick, days and years,
Tick, tick, smiles and tears.
Tick, tick, wind and wave,
Tick, tick, grief, the grave.

THE HEAD AND THE HEART.

The Head and the Heart had a quarrel one day,
　As to which was at fault for the other;
The Head with great arrogance always would say
　That the Heart was a wild, reckless brother.

And the Heart would not listen to reason;
　Yet it worked brave and strong all the hours,
While the Head tossed about in high treason
　As it talked on the nature of flowers.

And the heart with its warm pulsation
　Made many a grievous mistake,
But 'twas always on side of salvation
　For the poor fallen woman, or Rake.

The Head was a dastard old miser,
　Who doubted the whole of mankind,
And told the poor heart to be wiser
　And leave its pulsations for mind.

But the brave Heart replied in its glory,
　I would rather be fooled now and then
Than list to your cold, cynic story
　And doubt all my good fellow-men.

The Head was a ready-cash banker,
   While the Heart was a Prodigal Son,
And though his fair form grew lanker,
   His truth and his love weighed a ton.

If you met him in anguish or sorrow,
   In the walks of Vanity Fair,
A shilling or pound you could borrow,
   And his smile could be found everywhere.

But the selfish old Head turned coldly,
   And vaunted its pelf and its pride,
As he passed by his fellows so boldly,
   Where they starved, and they bled, and they died.

But old age struck this top-heavy creature,
   And left him alone with his tears;
Not a friend to gaze on his feature
   As he sank to his grave without tears.

Yet the noble old Heart with its failing,
   Had the prayers of the poor and the just,
And a funeral train all bewailing,
   When it passed to the sad, silent dust.

TRUTH AND LOVE.

The works of man shall crumble and decay,
His boast in brass and bronze shall pass away;
But o'er the rolling years of tide and time
The truth shall flourish in immortal prime.

Temples and towers shall crumble into dust,
Silver and gold shall perish with the rust—
And all things that we see below, above,
Shall vanish from the earth but lasting love.

The splendid wrecks of pyramids and thrones
Can only mark the spot where human bones
Still moulder into dust without a name—
The vain memorials of presumptive fame!

But truth, and love, and hope, and glorious song
Shall triumph over ages, and o'er wrong,
And cheer the drooping spirit through the night
When vice and vengeance battle with the right.

THIRTY YEARS.

[A memory of Mount Sterling, Ky.]

Thirty years are gone tomorrow
   Since these streams and hills I knew;
Thirty years of joy and sorrow
   Brings me back, dear hills, to you.

Many friends I loved are sleeping
   On the crest of yonder hill;
'Neath the willows gently weeping,
   Near the sound of Perry's mill.

Beaux and beauties that I cherished
   Left me in their early bloom,
Yet their memory never perished
   With the blight that blurs the tomb.

Raven locks no more are shining;
   Lost and gone the flowers of May;
Yet how vain is all repining
   In my crown of silver gray.

Vanished voices in the twilight
   Float above the hill and plain;
Call me fondly to the skylight,
   Thrill my heart with love again.

THE RISING SUN.

Shine out, thou glorious sun, upon a sleeping world
   And thrill the soul with fires from above—
Where thunderbolts are forged and flashed and hurled
   By one Almighty hand—source of light and love.

Arise, and stride across the ocean billow,
   And light thy pathway o'er the vales and hills,
Go, shine where beauty dreams upon her pillar
   And sparkles in the leaping mountain rills.

Let stars and moons and planets in their sweeping
   Pale their light before the splendid sway,
While I my weary matin watch am keeping
   To catch the glory of the God of day.

THE BOAST OF BACCHUS.

[Dedicated to the memories of "Bobby" Burns, Oliver Goldsmith, and Edgar Allen Poe.]

I reign over land, I reign over sea,
The proudest of earth I bring to my knee
As weak as a child in the midnight of care;
The prince and the peasant I strip bleak and bare.

A taste of my blood sends a thrill to the heart,
And speeds through the soul like a poisonous dart;
While I leave it a wreck of trouble and pain
That never on earth can be perfect again.

The youth in his bloom and the man in his might
I capture by day and I conquer by night;
The maid and the matron respond to my call,
I rule like a tyrant and ride over all.

In the gilded saloon and glittering crowd
I deaden the senses and humble the proud,
And tear from the noble, the good, and the great
The love and devotion of home, church, and state.

I blast all the honor that manhood holds dear,
I smile with delight at the sight of a tear,
And laugh in the revel and rout of a night;
My mission on earth is to blur and to blight.

I ruin the homes of the high and the low,
I blast every hope of the friend and the foe;
The world I sear with my blistering breath,
And millions I lead to the portals of death.

In the parlor and dance-house I sparkle and roar
Like billows that break on a wild, rocky shore;
I crush every virtue, destroy every truth
That blossoms in beauty or blushes in youth.

My power is mighty for sin and despair;
I crouch, like a lion that waits in his lair,
To mangle the life of the pure and the brave,
And drag them in sorrow to shame and the grave!

THE BATTLE OF SHILOH.

[Dedicated to the American soldier.]

Bands were playing, horses neighing,
Soldiers straying, mules were braying;
Banners flying, women crying,
Hearts were sighing, many dying;
Onward, backward, all uproarious,
The "Gray" victorious, the "Blue" was glorious.
The field was won, the field was lost,
Like ocean billows, torn and tossed;
And on the bloody beach of war
Waves of dead, a giant scar;
And mangled bodies torn and pale,
Like forests in a withering gale.
Up the hill and down the vale,
Advance, retreat, but never fail;
Fix bayonets, forward, guide right!
A shout, a yell, God! what a sight.
At them again through smoke and fire;
Fight and fall, but ne'er retire.
Once more to the breach, steady, strike—
Blood, broken bones, who saw the like
Never forgets through the long years
That call up our smiles and our tears.
Capture cannon, capture men,
Crash, smash, at them again.
Hark to the yell of Cleburne's men,
They rush like demons through the glen,
Driving the "Blue" toward the river,
And many are lost forever;
Sherman shouts "Halt! right about, charge!"
Then down through the brush and the gorge
The "Gray" in turn are flying.
Lord! how the soldiers are dying.
McClernand, McCook stand at bay,
While Wallace is lost on the way
To the field, where Prentiss surrenders

To the South and its brave defenders.
Cheatham, Withers, Gibson, and Bragg
Stand out like a wild, rocky crag
And beat back the bold invaders;
At last they are crushed by the raiders.
Then Crittenden, Hurlbut, and Wood
With many brave heroes withstood—
Charge after charge, through the rain
Of bullets that whizzed o'er the plain.
Webster shouts, "Park and unlimber!"
Shot and shell right through the timber—
Cannons that growl like December,
Sounds that we long shall remember,
Shriek like the roar from a burning hell!
Sending the foe to the rear pell-mell!
Danger and death so fierce and hard
To the halting troops of Beauregard!
Sunday's sun has gone at last,
Rushing rains are falling fast
On the faces cold as lead,
On the dying and the dead.
Brave Sidney Johnston led the "Gray,"
But Fate cut off his life that day,
And Beauregard could not repel
The Union fire—a blast from hell,
Where cannon thundered o'er the glen
And shattered horses, boys, and men.
Then Monday's sun arose in a gloom
And spread its clouds above this tomb,
Where Grant and Buell joined to smash
The stubborn Gray with one dread crash.
But still the Gray declined to yield,
And fought like tigers on the field—
Till wave on wave "the boys in blue"
Rolled o'er these Southern hearts so true—
While Sherman over swamp and bridge
Dashed on the gallant Breckinridge!
The day was won, the day was lost,
And twenty thousand told the cost,
Where brothers bled and brothers died—
A ruin with its crimson tide,
That flowed for you and flowed for me

On the torn banks of the Tennessee!
The sun goes down, the stars are set,
That bloody field we can't forget
While valor holds a deathless sway
And honor crowns the "Blue" and "Gray."
It may be that the winking "stars"
Contain the men who loved the "bars"—
And that those gallant, noble types
Join hands with those who loved the stripes.
But "stars" and "bars" and "red" and "blue"
And "stripes" and "stars" wave over you;
Our Nation fills our fame today—
The "red" is "Blue" and the "blue" is "**Gray**"!

    A thousand years of glory
        Shall immortalize our fame—
    With a tale in song and story
        To keep green the hallowed name
    Of the victor and the vanquished
        On the land and on the sea,
    A band of noble brothers
        Led by gallant Grant and Lee.
    And the tears of beaming beauty
        Shall freshen every flower—
    In the May-time of our duty,
        Through the sunlit, fleeting hour.
    Then we'll strew the rarest roses
        O'er the graves we bless today,
    And we'll pluck the purest posies
        To enwreath the "Blue" and "Gray."
    And down the circling ages,
        From the father to the son,
    We'll tell on golden pages
        How the field was lost and won;
    And how a band of brothers
        Fought each other hard and true
    To bind the Union arches
        O'er the "Gray" and o'er the "Blue,"
    And reared a lasting temple
        So complete in every plan,
    To justice, truth, and mercy
        And the liberty of man!

SUBLIMITY.

[Dedicated to Eugene Field.]

I hear in the voice of the thunder
  The glory and greatness of God;
I see in the flash of the lightning
  The sweep of my glittering rod.

I feel in the rush of the rain
  The flow of His melting tears,
And hear in the midnight winds
  The music of all the spheres.

I see in the limitless ocean
  The swell of His heaving breast,
And the hour is near when I shall
  Sink to His bosom of infinite rest.

CLEOPATRA'S REPLY.

[Dedicated to Gen. William Haynes Lytle, author of "I'm Dying, Egypt, Dying."]

I am dying, Antony, dying,
Yet I long for one embrace
To entwine my arms around you,
And still greet you face to face;
Ere I cross the stygian river
Testing highest heaven or hell,
I am pining for thy presence—
Come, and kiss a fond farewell.

I am dying, Antony, dying,
While the conquering hosts of Rome
Batter down my palace portals
And despoil my royal home;
Like great Cæsar's dashing legions
Rule the land and rule the sea,
I defy his sharpest torture—
You and Love rule only me.

I am dying, Antony, dying,
Yet, my soul-lit love forbids
To quench great furnace fires

Burning 'neath the pyramids
Of passion's deep foundation,
Laid by nature and her laws,
That abide by blood and impulse
From some great eternal cause.

I am dying, Antony, dying,
Yet, the "splendors of my smile"
Shall light thy pathway onward
To some grand celestial Nile,
Where among bright heavenly bowers
We shall clasp with magic might,
Crowned with everlasting flowers
Blooming always, day and night.

Come, my lion-hearted hero
To the jungles of my heart,
Feed upon the upland hillocks,
Never more to pine or part;
Wander grandly to the valley
Where the springs of life abound,
Cool the ardor of thy passion
In dark grottoes under ground.

GOLDEN HAIR.

[Dedicated to Emily Thornton Charles.]

Only a lock of golden hair
  That I gaze on with ceaseless pain,
Worn by an image pure and fair,
  That never shall bless me again.

She went like the mist of morning
  To shine with the stars above,
A beautiful, chaste adorning
  In a realm of endless love.

Yet often when evening twilight
  Encircles my heart with gloom
I hear her voice from the starlight
  That sparkles within my room.

And I see through the mystic moonbeams,
  Her form so rare and fair,
A radiant light from Heaven so bright,
  With tresses of golden hair.

LAURA.

Where the purple hills lie sleeping,
   Beneath the autumn shade,
And the trees are sadly weeping
   Their tribute o'er the glade;
There I laid my lovely Laura
   In days so long ago,
When my heart was full of sorrow
   As the mountains full of snow.

I've tried oft to forget her
   In the whirl of busy life,
But the more do I regret her
   In my round of daily strife;
And when evening shadows lower
   O'er the purple hills afar,
I recall the lonely hour
   When I lost my polar star.

Yet, the day is surely coming
   When we'll clasp with magic might,
Where the angel choirs are humming—
   In the bright celestial light—
Where the waters ever sparkle
   On that bright, eternal shore,
And our hearts will never darkle,
   But shall love for evermore.

MY SOUL AND SELF.

[Dedicated to Col. De Witt C. Sprague.]

My soul and self walked hand in hand
   Discoursing of the time to be,
When we should view the "Promised Land"
   And sink into eternity.

The Star of Hope was in my sky,
   And Faith reigned monarch of the hour,
While Love and Truth were always nigh
   To cheer me in their rosy bower.

I asked my sighing soul to tell
    The secret that enwraps the tomb,
Or if there was a burning hell
    To torture in eternal gloom.

I heard an echo faint and low,
    Come sounding o'er the wreck of years—
A voice all tremulous with woe
    That left me to my silent tears.

Dread silence brooded o'er my heart
    And brought a chaos of despair;
My soul and self then tore apart,
    With nothing here and nothing there!

"I HAVE SINNED AND I HAVE SUFFERED."

[Last words of John Howard Payne, author of "Home, Sweet Home.]

I have sinned and I have suffered,
    Yet the world will never know
How I tried to do my duty
    In the long, the long ago.

I have sinned and I have suffered,
    Human nature is so weak—
Yet my tongue cannot be tempted
    To disclose, betray, or speak.

I have sinned and I have suffered;
    Who has not through blood and bone?
If there be a mortal living,
    Let him bravely cast the stone.

I have sinned and I have suffered,
    Just the same as other men,
But my heart cannot be conquered,
    Nor the soul that burns within.

I have sinned and I have suffered;
    Mournful memories come to me;
Yet beyond the clouds of sorrow
    Rifts of sunshine I can see.

I have sinned and I have suffered,
    He can sink and He can save
All the human hearts that wander
    To the cold and silent grave.

THE OLD YEAR.

[Dedicated to Anonymous.]

Farewell, old year, we soon must sigh and sever;
  Another moment and you're lost to sight;
Yet in my heart I'll keep your form forever;
  And now, old friend, I bid you sweet good-night.

You've left some scars upon my aching heart,
  And robbed me of a dear and valued friend,
Sweet Love, who promised never more to part,
  Has passed away and come unto an end.

But even 'mong the joys you rudely shattered
  There shine some jewels that you can't destroy,
While memory still remains unbattered
  And heavenly hope is there without alloy.

Your keen-edged scythe has cut down many a beauty,
  O'er land and sea wherever you have trod,
Yet if their hands and hearts stuck close to duty
  I know they've gone to glory and their God.

And still I know the new year holds some pleasure
  For those who work and love their fellow-men,
While summer fields will yield their golden treasure
  When sunny skies shall shine for us again.

So fare thee well, my dear old wrinkled hero;
  The midnight clock rings out your funeral knell,
And soon you'll be as dead as tyrant Nero,
  But once again I sound a sweet farewell.

MORNING AND EVENING.

[Dedicated to Col. Will L. Visscher.]

In the morning of life I was filled with ambition
  To roam o'er the world and see sights afar;
But somehow in age I am prone to contrition
  At missing the splendors I saw in my star.

Many friends came around me in moments of pleasure
  Who drank at my banquet and laughed at my wit;
But when I had lost all my health and my treasure
  They left me alone in my sorrow to sit.

The voice of the crowd, as it rung in my praises,
　　Awakened a joy I imagined would last;
But, alas! my ambition lies under the daisies,
　　And the wrecks of my glory are strewn in the past.

No more shall I sail on the bright, bounding billow,
　　Where youth in its beauty rode high on the wave,
For soon shall I sleep 'neath the turf and the willow
　　And go to the millions that rest in the grave.

This tress of brown hair that I keep in my sorrow
　　And the withered remains of a beautiful rose
Shall shine o'er the ashes of hope every morrow,
　　And bring to my lone heart sweet peace and repose.

At the shrine of a memory I loved in my childhood
　　I kneel and I pray in the midnight of care,
And flit back again to the flowers in the wildwood,
　　While soaring in silence o'er grief and dispair.

Ah! who has not left still some sweet consolation
　　To soften the pangs and the thorns of regret,
When every wild fancy and dark devastation
　　In vain bids us banish the past and forget?

A MEMORY.

[Dedicated to DeLancy Gill.]

Adown the vanished years where mem'ry lingers
　　There comes to me a picture from the past,
And round her brow I see fond fairy fingers
　　Entwining rarest roses to the last.

Her laughing voice could banish every sorrow;
　　Her sunny smile was all the world to me—
Yet vainly from the past I try to borrow
　　Her presence from that dark eternity.

It must be that beyond the stars now shining
　　She waits and watches for my coming call;
For oft in dreams my weary head reclining,
　　Upon her bosom finds its sweet enthrall.

THE OCEAN GRAVE.

Let me rest in the boundless ocean,
    Where the storm-king rules the wave,
Where waters are ever in motion
    Above a limitless grave.

Let me rest where the roaring billow
    Resounds o'er the waters wide,
A dirge o'er my coral pillow
    A song for my mermaid bride.

Let me rest where the evening twilight
    Mellows the parting day,
Where the sea-birds flit in the moonlight
    Through breakers of blue and gray.

Let me sink where the sands are shining
    On the surf of a lonely shore,
Where the clouds have a silver lining
    And there's rest for evermore.

A DOLLAR OR TWO.

[Dedicated to the Washington Lodge of Elks.]

With circumspect steps as we pick our way thro'
This intricate world, as all prudent folks do,
May we still on our journey be able to view
The benevolent face of a dollar or two.
For an excellent thing is a dollar or two;
No friend is so true as a dollar or two.
    In country or town, as we pass up and down,
We are cock of the walk with a dollar or two.

Do you wish to escape from the bachelor crew
And a charming young innocent female to woo
You must always be ready the handsome to do
Although it may cost you a dollar or two.
For love tips his darts with a dollar or two;
Young affections are gained by a dollar or two;
    And beyond all dispute the best card of your suit
Is the eloquent chink of a dollar or two.

Do you wish to have friends who your bidding will do,
And help you your means to get speedily through,
You'll find them remarkably faithfully true
By the magical power of a dollar or two.
For friendship's secured by a dollar or two;
Popularity's gained by a dollar or two.
   And you'll n'er want a friend till you've no more to lend
And yourself need to borrow a dollar or two.

*Do you wish in the courts of the country to sue
For the right or estate that's another man's due,
Your lawyer will surely remember his cue
When his palm you have crossed with a dollar or two.
For a lawyer's convinced with a dollar or two,
And a jury set right with a dollar or two.
   And though justice *is* blind, yet a way you can find
To open his eyes with a dollar or two.

If a claim that is proved to be honestly due,
Department or Congress you'd quickly put through,
And the chance for its payment begins to look blue,
You can help it along with a dollar or two.
For votes are secured by a dollar or two,
And influence bought by a dollar or two;
   And he'll come to grief who depends for relief
Upon justice not braced with a dollar or two.

Do you wish that the press should the decent thing do
And give your reception a gushing review,
Describing the dresses by stuff, style, and hue,
On the quiet, hand Jenkins a dollar or two.
For the pen sells its praise for a dollar or two,
And flings its abuse for a dollar or two.
   And you'll find that it's easy to manage the crew
When you put up the shape of a dollar or two.

Do you wish your existence with faith to imbue,
And so become one of the sanctified few;
Who enjoy a good name and a well-cushioned pew,
You must really come down with a dollar or two.
For the gospel is preached for a dollar or two;
Salvation is reached for a dollar or two;
   Sins are pardoned sometimes, but the worst of all crimes
Is to find yourself short of a dollar or two.
   *Anonymous.

Do you wish to get into a game with the crew
Who sport on the "green" with the "red," "white," and "blue."
In a small game of draw where your chances are few,
You must back up your talk with a dollar or two.
For the "dealer" is "fly" with a dollar or two,
And the "banker" is "flush" with a dollar or two;
   And whate'er you say, they won't let you play
Unless you come down with a dollar or two.

Should you "hanker" for Wall street as Gentile or Jew,
Where the "bulls" and "bears" wait for "gudgeons" like you,
Your pile they will measure and take into view,
And scoop with a smile your last dollar or two.
For the "bull" is rampant for a dollar or two,
And the "bear" ever growls for a dollar or two;
   Yet, I'll say on my oath that the broker rules both
And seldom gets left on his dollar or two.

Do you want a snug place where there's little to do,
Civil service evade and its rules to break through,
A land bill to pass or a patent renew—
You can fix the thing up with a dollar or two;
For Commissions can see through a dollar or two;
Even Congressmen wink at a dollar or two,
   And you need not be slow to convince friend or foe
Of the virtue contained in a dollar or two!

MAN.

I met him yesterday in lusty health,
   Surrounded with the strength of pomp and power,
But all the train that waited on his wealth
   Could not insure him life one single hour.

Today I saw him coffined and confined
   Within a narrow cell beneath the sod,
With all his earthly prospects there resigned,
   Dependent on the mercy of his God.

Tomorrow's sun shall set upon his fame,
   And leave no trace of where he lived or died,
While even the record of his wealth and name
   Shall vanish with his power and his pride!

LORD BYRON.

[Dedicated to James Whitcomb Riley, the Hoosier Poet.]

Immortal bard! thy glorious, royal thought
Sprung from thy brain, Minerva-like and caught
The echoes of the fleeting, rolling years
That thrill the music of the sounding spheres.
Proud, independent, and still a stoic,
Always grand, peculiar, and heroic—
Who looked upon the hypocrites of earth
As crawling worms, unworthy of a birth,
Who only left their slime upon their day,
Were unremembered when they passed away.
Small creatures who are fitted for poor pelf
Who live and die in concentrated self!
But thou, an eagle from some Alpine peak
Bathing its plumage in the cloud-capped foam,
Wandering o'er this world, to vainly seek
For truth and love, for honest heart and home.
Beneath Italian skies you sought for peace,
And steered your bounding bark round isles of Greece,
Along the shores of Oriental lands,
Where billows break upon their golden sands.
And o'er the desert wild you loved to roam,
But never found on earth a rest or home.
Giaour, the Venitian, made Hassan bleed
And cleft his head upon the prancing steed,
All for the love he bore sweet Lelia dead—
Where ocean billows broke above her head.
'Tis sweet to be revenged on dastard man
And kill a hated tyrant when you can,
Who knows no law within, below, above—
Dark, brutal passion only felt for love!
Now, see the Giaour in his death-bed trance
Clasp lovely Lelia with his parting glance.
Confessed his crimes, defiant of his course
And died without a pang or feeling of remorse;
A lone and broken wreck upon the shore
A brave and royal spirit evermore.
One who could face the shades of death so well,
Defying all the powers of earth and hell.

The bride of Abydos you brightly paint
In colors that Old Time can never taint;
Her love as constant as the polar star
That shines o'er Arctic night so fair and far,
And for the youthful Selim she defied
A parent's terror and the world beside.
Who pledged her happiness, her love in strife,
A shining rainbow in the storms of life,
Who, when her lover, forced to die and part,
Could rend her soul, one sigh, a broken heart!
Zaleika; from thy cyprus mount on high
Above the billow, near Hellenic sky,
The bulbul and the nightingale doth sing
A requiem as their mighty offering
To one who loved not wisely, but too well,
Thou paragon of beauty, fare thee well.
Within the cell of Tasso we may find
The wreck and ruin of a brilliant mind,
Who loved beyond his rank and wand'ring state
Leonora, the princess and ingrate,
Who, like Alphonso, the mean tyrant duke,
Could calmly look on wrong and not rebuke.
Yet all the glories of the house of Este
Have long since vanished like a fearful pest,
While Tasso and his lovelit lines shall shine
Along the rolling years, supreme, divine!
Byron, 'lone, proud, and friendless everywhere
Except when sailing with thine own Corsair,
Conrad, the pirate, and his queenly care.
The lovelit homicide, the wild Gulnare!
Yet, in the tower with sweet Medora dead
You lay upon her breast your aching head,
And from those wild eyes tears of truth o'erflow
The sparkling messenger of nameless woe.
But, quickly, all these signs of grief depart,
" In helpless, hopeless, brokenness of heart!"
Childe Harold, thou licentious Don Juan,
Yet not myself in all that thou dost plan,
"To point a moral and adorn a tale,"
For secret scoundrels, hypocrites so frail
Who know themselves as villians, dastard liars,
Dreading man's detection, perdition fires,

Who only prate and preach and never feel
The glorious impulse of a grand ideal!
And I have searched the quarry of thy thought
For marbles rare, uncovered and unbought,
And delved into thy mind, so sad and lone
To find in depths the prisoner of Chillon,
Who dungeoned, for sweet liberty and truth,
The tyrant's portion—for heroic youth.
That would not yield till all his kindred slept
Beneath the prison stones where he hath wept
To hear his brothers in their clanking chains
Die with moaning, groans, and patient pains.
Homer, Shakspeare, to thee alone compare,
Godlike triumvirate, grand, rich, and rare,
Shall shine through all the ages and all time,
The life of virtue and the death of crime!
And, oh! sweet Bard, where'er Augusta lies
And faithful friendship turns to thee her eyes,
There, from the earth the tribute of our tears
Shall melt like dewdrops in the coming years,
And o'er your hallowed dust we'll send a sigh
For one immortal soul that cannot die!

A CONFEDERATE SOLDIER.

[To the memory of Thos. J. Luttrell.]

A manly man has passed away,
  He rests beneath the silent sod.
He carried sunshine in his day,
  And gave his heart and soul to God.

In war and peace he was so brave,
  Kept duty as his guide and chart,
Although his body fills the grave,
  His memory lingers in the heart.

Peace to his ashes, rest his soul;
  No more his smiling face we'll see;
He's reached at last the final goal,
  And shines within eternity.

DON'T!

Don't quarrel with what you can't help,
   For this life is not very long;
Don't listen to every whelp
   That barks at your heels, right or wrong.

Don't worry when friends shall betray,
   They've done it since Judas began;
Hold truth in the night or the day,
   And then, you will feel like a man!

Don't look for perfection below,
   For all that is mortal must sin,
And each one is subject to woe,
   No matter how pure he's within.

Don't fear to go under the sod;
   To die is no more than be born,
Have trust in yourself and your God
   And you'll meet in some heavenly morn!

TRIUMPHANT.

[Dedicated to Col. D. B. Henderson, Dubuque, Iowa.]

Though conquered and bleeding and dying,
   My spirit soars high o'er the gale,
And round me sweet voices are sighing
   A dirge for the noble who fail.

Long lines of the conquered are coming
   To waft me away to the skies,
And echoes are peacefully humming
   A song for the hero who dies—

For the rights he has fervently cherished
   Along the dark vale of despair,
And for his own truth he has perished
   Like dewdrops that melt into air.

No marble may mark his cold ashes,
   No song lend a charm to his name;
The lightning of war only flashes
   The death moan that murmurs his fame.

The grass grows as green o'er the conquered
    As where the victorious lie;
They fell with a yell for a watchword
    That taught their proud manhood to die.

When God comes to judge all His creatures
    Who toddle through life's little day,
I know he will mark his own features
    In the mortal that falls by the way.

And when victory garlands her heroes
    Who perish in naked detail,
She will not crown the long line of Neros,
    But the truthful who struggle and fail!

THE JEW.

[Dedicated to the fair Hebrew ladies.]

The wild ivy vine of old Palestine
    Creeps over its temple and towers
And leaves but a trace of the historic race
    That once filled its beautiful bowers.

Yet age after age on every page
    Of the record of love and of life,
The Hebrew appears to bloom o'er the years
    And soars over sorrow and strife.

Though crushed and reviled, defeated, despoiled,
    The seed of the martyrs abound,
And all o'er the earth where mortals have birth
    The Jew and the Jewess are found.

In science and art they each take a part,
    And labor for liberty, too;
The tyrant they hate in church or in state,
    And freedom they always pursue.

Success to the Jew, the wandering Hebrew,
    Who never was known to despair;
In bondage or chains, in losses or pains,
    His face can be seen everywhere.

WHEN LOVE IS DEAD.

[Dedicated to the memory of Frank Schwartz.]

When love is dead, with all the hopes we cherished,
    What matters every scene of fleeting life?
Far better to be with the loved ones perished
    Than linger longer through this warring strife.

When love is dead the world is all a blank,
    From rise of sun to evening's golden glow;
Nor wealth nor power, nor all the joys of rank
    Can ease the heart for love lost long ago.

There's nothing left to cheer the wounded heart,
    Except what memory calls its own;
And that is often like a poisoned dart
    That chills the soul when we are left alone.

Yet, far beyond the sun and shining stars,
    There must be rest and joy for those who sigh,
Where love eternal knows no cruel scars,
    And where affection cannot doubt or die!

A SPRAY.

[To the memory of Gustave A. Forsberg, artist.]

I place a spray upon thy cold, dead form,
    To memory and the wilds of long ago;
And think of thee in sunshine and in storm,
    As rhythmic music with its fluent flow.

The time we spent in magic, midnight hours,
    Where art and beauty led the truant train,
Have vanished with the bright and fading flowers
    That ne'er shall thrill our wandering lives again.

But, in my heart I cherish all your glory,
    And o'er your coffined manhood shed a tear;
While life remains I'll sound your genial story,
    And tell your pleasant tales from year to year.

SHALL WE LIVE AGAIN?

[Dedicated to Hon. William B. Allison, U. S. Senator.]

I asked the hills in vernal bloom
To tell me if beyond the tomb
The mind of man is full and free,
The heir to all eternity.

I asked the seas, that grandly roll
Their wrinkled brows from pole to pole,
If far beyond their utmost shore
There is a life for evermore.

I asked the stars, that nightly shine
As jewels in the crown divine,
If man shall live within their sphere,
Devoid of all the dross that's here.

I asked the sun, whose heavenly light
Shines somewhere always day and night,
To tell me if the soul of man
Exists beyond this little span.

The hills and seas, and stars and sun
Made glorious answer one by one,
Proclaiming with a grand refrain—
"*God wills that man shall live again!*"

THE POET.

You'll bury his body, but not his thought,
   For thousands of years to come;
And he'll live in the works his brain has wrought
   When temples and statues are dumb.

For he teaches the lesson of ages
   To all the schools of mankind—
That old truth, with its golden pages,
   Is the essence of magic mind.

And his songs shall sound o'er the rolling years
   To the tune of eternal time,
And echo along through celestial spheres
   With the bliss of angelic rhyme.

SHED NO TEARS.

[Dedicated to my wife.]

Shed no tears when I am gone,
   Cease thy earthly sorrow;
Find again some fairer one,
   Love again tomorrow.

Shed no tears, for tears are vain,
   To bring back the departed;
Who lived in keen, pathetic pain,
   And died—the broken hearted.

Shed no tears, let sunshine fill
   The measure of thy life;
Wander like a sparkling rill,
   Away from sin and strife.

Shed no tears above my clay,
   But lay me 'neath the willow,
Where the morning sunbeams play
   Above my pulseless pillow.

Shed no tears, but in some hour
   Go kneel beside my grave;
Plant a bright, carnation flower,
   And lonely let it wave.

Then, turn away, but shed no tears,
   And seek the banquet hall;
Where you may shine throughout the years,
   The pride and joy of all!

THE EAGLE.

[Dedicated to Columbia.]

Who taught you how to soar so high,
   And wander in the upper blue?
Why can't I float along the sky
   And be a mate with storms and you?
I've seen you from grand rocky heights
   Sail proudly on your tireless wing,
And bathe your plumage in the lights

Where you have ruled, as battle king.
Your shoreless realm is broad and free,
   Without a limit here below,
And reaches to eternity,
   Where heavenly waters flash and flow.
How well you typify the force
   Of nature and her royal plan,
The form and power and strength and source
   Of all that's great in tyrant man.
On Alpine crags in winter hours
   Your flashing eye defies the sun,
And battles with the stormy powers
   Till nature and her laws are won.
You rob the hills so far away,
   Where reigns the wolf and stalwart stag,
To feed your brood at close of day,
   That hunger on the mountain crag.
And in the rosy rays of dawn
   I've heard your wild and piercing scream,
When dashing on the famished fawn
   While drinking at the sparkling stream.
Oh! could I fly and sail with you,
   Where Freedom holds her splendid sway
Among the stars that gem the blue,
   And lights up an eternal day!

APOSTROPHE TO OLD OCEAN.

[The Grave of Untold Millions.]

Uprear your hills of emerald spray,
And drown mankind that sail today.
Engulf them in your gloomy grave,
Where coral branches lonely wave.
Leave no memorial where they died,
But revel in your royal pride.
Millions of years you've reigned alone,
A mighty monarch on your throne.
And how you roll and rave and roar
Against the rocks upon the shore,
Destroying islands in your course—
A tyrant power without remorse.

Great lands have sunk beneath your tread,
Enwrapping millions with the dead.
You shriek o'er those you now entomb,
Who vanished in their brilliant bloom,
And roar their dirge with ceaseless strain,
Demanding more to still enchain
Within your hungry mammoth maw,
The emblem of eternal law!
Vain are the powers of man to stay
Your gnawing grasp so cold and gray
That earthquake shocks cannot retire
Or ruin with volcanic fire.
Your tidal waves reach high and grand
To devastate the ling'ring land;
And how you laugh with thund'ring joy
When us weak mortals you destroy.
Forever roll from pole to pole,
Thou tyrant god without a soul;
From arctic snow to tropic sun,
The glory of that Mystic One,
Who times the tide from land to land,
And holds the waters in His hand.
Encircle all the earth with fear
And be the terror of the year;
Uprear your broad-back billows high,
Defy the clouds and storms and sky,
And challenge all that sin or sigh
To come to thee, lament and die!

GENIUS.

[Dedicated to Leo Wheat, of Virginia.]

He thrills the heart with grand, poetic numbers,
   And plucks the crown of thorns from brows of care;
He wakes and thinks what time the sluggard slumbers,
   And scatters gems of beauty everywhere.

Entrancing music with voluptuous swell
   He casts upon the weary, mystic mind,
Sounding as sweetly as some far-off bell,
   Evolving hope and love for all mankind.

The canvas glows beneath his magic hand
  With forms of grace, and grace that is divine;
He pictures all the gems of sea and land,
  Securing to the world the superfine.

His chisel carves the marble into form
  Of bust and statue, pyramid and tower,
Defying ages of both sun and storm
  To crush the thought that thrilled him for an hour.

And yet the Genius with his suffering soul
  Oft wanders o'er the earth misunderstood
By chattering daws who never reach the goal
  Of knowing how to do their fellows good.

But when he's seen no more in field or town,
  And all his mortal part lies cold and dead,
Some sage or city for their self-renown,
  Will give a shaft where once he needed bread!

THE DYING YEAR.

The year is dying, the winds are sighing
  Amid the forest branches cold and gray,
While snows are falling and crows are calling
  Their mates in chorus through the cloudy day.

I pause and ponder and weirdly wander
  Among the years that slumber in the past,
Where friends have vanished with pleasure banished,
  While vainlike visions haunt me to the last.

That dead December I well remember
  When dear bright beauties beamed upon my life,
And every treasure brought double pleasure
  Before I lost my loving child and wife.

And yet the roses and perfumed posies
  Will bloom again above their vernal sod,
Where Hope still lingers with rosy fingers
  To point us to the glory of our God.

THE CLICK OF THE CLOCK.

[To an Old Clock.]

Every click of the clock lessens life's little span,
    And blots out the hopes of an hour,
With all the ambitions of vain little man
    Who struts in his pride and his power.

Every tick of the clock drives us on to the end
    Of the road through the journey of life,
While out of the line falls friend after friend
    Away from all sorrow and strife.

Every stroke of the clock in the midnight of care
    Sounds solemn and dreary and lone,
While the heart grows so weary, so barren and bare,
    Beating on to the dark, great unknown.

Our days are soon numbered and soon we'll depart
    To the darkness encircling the tomb,
But while we remain let us cherish each heart
    And virtue that's ever in bloom.

Let us hope and believe that the spirit shall reign
    In a realm of love and of light,
Where dear ones shall clasp us again and again
    And everything rules for the right!

THE LONG AGO.

[Dedicated to Gen. James M. Ewing, Washington, D. C.]

Dear Jim, do you think of the long, long ago?
    When our hearts and our souls were all feeling,
And we knew not of sin, of sorrow, or woe
    When classmates at school in old Wheeling.

The years have flown fast; the cold winter blast
    Has furrowed our hearts and our features,
Yet the fate we endure is as certainly sure
    To come to all weak, human creatures.

Yet, as life runs along, we shall sing the "old song"
    Of Love, Truth, and Justice forever,
And wherever we be, on the land or the sea,
    No storm our friendship can sever.

We'll laugh and we'll think, and "sometimes" may drink
  To the friends that we knew in the dawning,
When life was so bright, every morn, noon, and night,
  And the heart never thought about fawning.

And when life is o'er, on some beautiful shore
  I hope we shall meet amid flowers
With the friends of our youth, whose beauty and truth
  Shall enliven sweet heavenly hours.

NAPOLEON.

A wreck of ambition, deserted, alone,
He rode o'er the bones of mankind to a throne:
Men, women, and nations were playthings to him,
A great goblet of blood he quaffed to the brim.
The faithful of France he slaughtered for fame,
While kings were his pawns and queens were his game;
His conquering eagles o'er Alpine snow,
Rushed down, like an avalanche, freighted with woe;
The fierce storms of old Moscow fanning its fire,
Compelled the invader to turn and retire,
And leave untold thousands to die in his track,
For vultures to feed on and Cossacks to hack.
The star of his destiny sunk out of view;
Eclipsed in the blood of his last Waterloo;
Then, exiled from France, his hope and his pride,
Caged like a lion he fretted and died.
A marvelous meteor that flashed o'er the wave,
To darkle at last in the gloom of the grave.
Far better, the lowest, poor peasant of France,
Who toils in his vineyard or joins in the dance,
Than all of his glory in battle array,
That, sooner or later, will vanish away.
Peace, virtue, and truth are the jewels of joy—
The hope of the world, without base alloy;
The gifts of our Maker, the best on this sod,
The glory of genius and tributes of God.
Vain, vain, all the pomp of Napoleon's high pride;
Broken-hearted, alone, disappointed, he died,
And left to the world but the sound of his name,
The fool of ambition, the football of fame!

THE ANSWER OF THE STARS.

[Dedicated to the memory of my dear daughter, Katie darling.]

I held her dead, cold hand in mine.
  Then gazed upon her folded eyes,
And asked her for a single sign
  To guide me to the heavenly skies.

I smoothed her gentle, lovely face
  And fixed the tresses on her brow;
I kissed her lips, like fretted lace,
  Still trusting she might answer now.

Yet she was dumb as marble stone,
  And left me lonely to repine;
I called her "darling," "sweet," "mine own,"
  But still she gave me not a sign.

I laid her in the dull, cold earth,
  Where roses bloom above her head,
And where the faithful have new birth
  In realms beyond, where none are dead.

I then appealed unto the stars,
  Those radiant eyes of God's domain—
When they replied o'er golden bars,
  "The good shall meet their own again!"

A TOAST TO ERIN.

[Dedicated to the memory of Robert Emmet.]

Here's to the land of the shamrock and myrtle,
  The land of the linnet, the lark, and the thrush;
Where always is heard the mourne of the turtle,
  That coos to his mate from the hawthorn bush.

Here's to the land of the glorious Emmet,
  Who fell in the front of fair Freedom's sweet cause;
The land of Wolf Tone, and love without limit,
  That tramples forever o'er tyranny's laws.

Here's to the land of great Goldsmith and Grattan,
  To Sheridan, Phillips, O'Connell, and Moore,
Whose brains shone as bright as sheen on the satin,
  Was filled with the riches of legendary lore.

Here's to the land of the roebuck and heather,
   The wild " Connaught Rangers " that never knew fear;
Who battle for freedom in fair or foul weather,
   And die for their country through year after year.

Here's to the bright Limerick lasses forever;
   The dear Dublin belles and the ladies of Cork;
Their hearts are so true that distance can't sever
   The songs they have sung with the notes of a lark.

Here's to the land of sweet songs and sad story;
   To exiles that roam o'er this cold, barren earth;
To men who have bled on battlefields gory,
   Successful for all but the land of their birth.

Here's to old Erin, the gem of the ocean,
   The land of the poet, the soldier, and sage;
Where eloquence burns with fire and emotion—
   Where liberty struggles from age unto age!

WE NEVER DIE!

We never die, and only step
   From sphere to sounding sphere,
Advancing ever forward
   Through one eternal year.

We never die, but only change
   This coat of crumbling clay
For garments ever brighter—
   For one celestial day.

We never die, we always lived
   In worlds before this earth;
Let's onward, onward ever
   To where the soul had birth.

We never die; there is no death!
   All nature teaches life,
The soul shall live forever
   Beyond this vale of strife.

O'ER THE EMBERS.

O'er the embers of departed pleasure
   I ponder lonely on the days no more,
And think of loved ones that I fondly treasure
   Who've long since landed on the other shore.

Their image beams from out the smoldering fire,
   Where memory holds her banquet to the last;
Their voices vibrate on the golden lyre
   That links the passing present with the past.

Again I hear their songs of bliss and beauty,
   Their merry laughter and their joyous glee,
When all was truth and hope and duty,
   And Life and Love were all the world to me.

And though the snows of many a cruel winter
   Have fallen thickly o'er my bending head,
And Time upon my brow has been a printer,
   I still must cherish the dear, sainted dead.

Well! I'll cover up the embers with the ashes
   Of fruitless efforts that have passed away,
And linger on the lights that memory flashes
   Across the fields now barren, bleak, and gray.

ARLINGTON.

A PROSE POEM—GRAPHIC DESCRIPTION OF THE NATIONAL CEMETERY.

[Dedicated to the Twenty-sixth National Encampment, G. A. R.; framed and hung up in soldier cemeteries, homes, and Grand Army posts.]

Arlington holds within her emerald bosom 17,000 heroic warriors. Like an Egyptian Queen in mournful majesty, gazing on the eternal waters of the Nile, Arlington rears her romantic head to the sky and bathes her feet in the murmuring waters of the Potomac.

The gnarled oak, the cedar, and sighing pine echo back the caw of the crow and the song of the wild bird, and through the morning sunlight and evening twilight the various voices of nature chant a requiem over the mouldering remains of our loyal dead.

This spot is dedicated to heroism. Its green sward is the mausoleum of patriotic hearts, its dome the bending heavens, and its altar candles the watching stars of God!

As the years glide away and coming centuries usher into life millions of human beings, Arlington shall be a Mecca for the unalterable principles of truth, and around its undulating vales and green hillocks the spirit of love and loyalty shall kneel at the vespers of Nationality and swing perfumed censors at the holy shrine of prayer and patriotism.

Monuments in marble, granite, and bronze lift their modest or pretentious heads, appealing to the memory of those who wander near the lowly bed where valor sleeps, but when these emblems of love and remembrance shall have passed away and crumbled into impalpable dust, the truth for which they died shall shine out like the rising sun and be as lasting as eternity.

The home of romance, wealth, and slavery has become at last the sepulcher of the dead, and the laughing, musical voices of the proud past are but a memory in the columned mansion of General Lee.

Sheridan, of the Army, and Porter, of the Navy, sleep their last sleep in front of Arlington mansion, and the Stars and Stripes floating from the tall staff throws its glinting shadows over the heroes that rest below.

Long, regimental lines of white headstones fade away into forest vistas, and Sheridan seems to ride down the valley, through Winchester, to turn retreat into victory.

Templed, unlike the Roman Pantheon, the divinities of Arlington are dedicated to patriotism, and its worshipers are a Christian people. From its columned porch the eye beholds to the east and north, across the Potomac, the mansions, temples, steeples, domes, and monuments of Washington and Georgetown, framed in by the rolling hills of Maryland. To the south and west the eye may linger on the historic Long Bridge and Alexandria, where the martyr Ellsworth lost his life for freedom.

In the dim distance a chain of forts and earthworks rear their crumbling heads. Thirty years of rains, snows, and suns have wrinkled their bald brows, yet Dame Nature, with her universal kindness, has covered the rude scars of war with the daisy, the the morning glory, and the Virginia creeper.

The ploughshare of industry has leveled down the red ridges of rebellion, and where once the reveille and long roll of battle resounded, the horn of the husbandman calls his toilers of peace from fields of waving grain and golden fruit to the rustic board of joy and love.

The brave hearts that slumber forever at Arlington, as well as those dear comrades at Shiloh, Chickamauga, Fredericksburg, and Gettysburg, dedicated their lives to liberty and immortalized their devotion by death. Who will care for their loved mounds when we are gone? Who will then strew roses and plant bright flowers in the May-time of nature? Other patriotic hands of brave men and fair women will take up the roll of duty, and even when all but liberty has perished from the earth the robin and the bluebird, the jay, and the mocking bird will warble at sunrise a reveille over the green sod that wraps their sacred clay. Nature herself will deck the graves of our fallen comrades, and the winds of Heaven will chant a requiem to their memory and kiss the loved spot where heroes slumber.

Thousands of loved comrades rest in unknown graves, far away from the loved ones at home. They sleep in a land of strangers, where the tears of love cannot moisten the green shroud that mantles their ashes. But if no kind hand is there to strew flowers, or loved eye to shed the tear of sorrow, there is One that reigns among the eternal stars that daily flood the unknown grave with sunshine and nightly water the budding wild flowers with dews from Heaven!

> Beside the river grave grasses quiver,
>   Where loyal hosts, their work have bravely done;
> They sleep in glory and live in story—
>   The martyred heroes of our Arlington.

Upon the ocean with deep devotion
  Our naval heroes fought with noble pride,
Sustained our banner in gallant manner,
  And for their country freely bled and died.

No more to battle where muskets rattle,
  And blood flowed free as water from a spring,
At rest forever beside the river—
  The nation's chalice with its offering!

The flag they fought for, the end they sought for,
  Shine grandly in the Union of today,
And no false reason or trumped up treason
  Can from its granite moorings cut away.

No sunlight streaming nor moonlight beaming
  Shall ever shine for these brave hearts again;
Their race is finished, yet undiminished,
  Their glory triumphs o'er the battle plain.

Unborn ages on golden pages
  Shall tell the story of their loyal cause,
And how they perished for rights they cherished
  Defending Freedom and her honest laws.

THE END.